"YOUR JOB IS *NOT* TO GROW A COMPANY. YOUR JOB IS TO GROW PEOPLE THAT GROW A COMPANY."

—JACK DALY

· ·

LOOKING
FORWARD
to MONDAY

ADAM WITTY

LOOKING
FORWARD
to MONDAY

How to

CREATE A WORKPLACE THAT **BREEDS GREATNESS,**
ATTRACTS AND RETAINS A-PLAYERS, AND **MAKES WORK FUN**

Advantage.

Published by Advantage, Charleston, South Carolina.
Member of Advantage Media Group.

ADVANTAGE is a registered trademark, and the Advantage colophon is a trademark of Advantage Media Group, Inc.

Printed in the United States of America.

10 9 8 7 6 5 4 3 2 1

ISBN: 978-1-64225-159-3
LCCN: 2018938583

Cover and layout design by George Stevens.

This publication is designed to provide accurate and authoritative information in regard to the subject matter covered. It is sold with the understanding that the publisher is not engaged in rendering legal, accounting, or other professional services. If legal advice or other expert assistance is required, the services of a competent professional person should be sought.

Advantage|ForbesBooks is proud to be a part of the Tree Neutral® program. Tree Neutral offsets the number of trees consumed in the production and printing of this book by taking proactive steps such as planting trees in direct proportion to the number of trees used to print books. To learn more about Tree Neutral, please visit **www.treeneutral.com**.

Advantage|ForbesBooks is a publisher of business, self-improvement, and professional development books. We help entrepreneurs, business leaders, and professionals share their Stories, Passion, and Knowledge to help others Learn & Grow. Do you have a manuscript or book idea that you would like us to consider for publishing? Please visit advantagefamily.com or call 1.866.775.1696.

This book is dedicated to every leader.
You have a noble and awesome role.
You have the opportunity to make a
positive difference in the life of every
person who works with you, to build
an organization where people say,
"I'm Looking Forward to Monday!"

Mark it up.
Dog-ear it.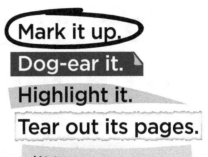
Highlight it.
Tear out its pages.

Wallpaper it with
sticky notes.

But whatever you do, don't *just* read it.

Merely *reading* a book suggests
a curl-up-by-the-fire affair.
But that's not what *Looking
Forward to Monday* is about.
These pages are jam-packed
with practical ideas that are
easy to implement.

Roll up your sleeves. Grab your
favorite pen and your brightest
highlighter. Dive in and fully
immerse. And don't stop until
these pages are tattooed
with notes, underlines and
exclamation points.

OTHER BOOKS BY ADAM WITTY

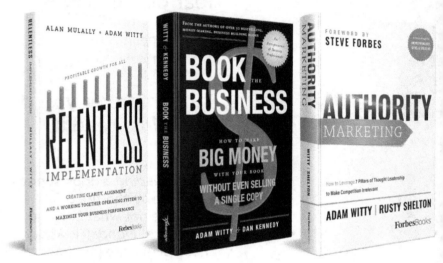

Relentless Implementation

Creating Clarity, Alignment, and a Working Together Operating System to Maximize Your Business Performance

Book the Business

How to Make Big Money with Your Book without Even Selling a Single Copy

Authority Marketing

How to Leverage 7 Pillars of Thought Leadership to Make Competition Irrelevant

TABLE OF CONTENTS

WHO A
AND W
SHOUL
CARE?

"THE OBJECT OF YOUR LIFE
IS TO MAKE YOUR VOCATION
YOUR VACATION."

—MARK TWAIN

WHO AM I AND WHY SHOULD YOU CARE?

AS AN ENTREPRENEUR AND CEO,

I have tremendous passion for business and also for growth. That's true of almost every entrepreneur and CEO I've ever met; it's the challenge that gets us into the office at 7 a.m., the challenge that keeps us there until 10 p.m., and the challenge that has us looking forward to Mondays and feeling sorry to see Friday afternoons come so quickly. It is the challenge of growth—growing our business to serve more customers, affect more people, and have more impact.

In my fifteen years as a CEO, I've learned, sometimes the hard way, that creating a work environment that breeds greatness—creating an environment where people look forward to Monday—is THE key to business growth. If you can get that recipe right in your business, then you won't work another day in your whole life, because work will be fun. Some call this *culture*. I don't care what you call it, as long as you make it happen.

So, who am I to tell you or even suggest that you might want to do things differently in your business? If you're an entrepreneur or CEO running a growth business, my story is probably similar to yours. I didn't grow up thinking I wanted to be an entrepreneur. I grew up in an entrepreneurial household; my father was an entrepreneur who discovered his own passion for business after what most people would see as a calamity, yet hitting this low point was actually the best thing that could have happened to him. He worked for a large, well-known company, but one day he walked in to find out that his job had been eliminated. After being down and out about it for a day or two, he said, "The heck with this. I can do what they do, and I can do it better." That idea inspired him and a colleague who had also been laid off to collaborate and start their own company. As a kid, I had the good fortune of witnessing my dad and his business partner create their startup company. My mom was their first employee, working as the receptionist and secretary. There was even a company dog, Cody, who lived in the garage, my entrepreneurial father's first office!

I saw my father grow that company from a garage with two people and a dog into a multimillion-dollar company with more than a hundred employees, a company that he and his partner would later sell for a sizeable sum. Seeing that up close and personal as a kid taught me that even the most daunting challenge can be turned into an opportunity. It also allowed me to witness the joys and triumphs and the fulfillment and gratification that come from growing a business, and from growing people within that business.

Even with that experience, I wasn't at all certain that I needed to start a business of my own. But I guess the apple didn't fall far from the tree; when I was in college, I got the idea to sell some of the tickets for Orlando Magic games that my family regularly bought but couldn't use. In 2001, I started a company called TicketAdvantage, a website to buy and sell sports tickets. I ran that company for the four years I was in college and grew it to a quarter of a million dollars in annual sales. It certainly paid for plenty of pizzas, but I was never able to scale it to a higher level.

When I graduated from Clemson, I'd learned that I LOVED business and entrepreneurship, and since several of my friends and professors told me I was "highly unemployable," it was clear to me I'd have to start something on my own. I was a few weeks out from graduation when I had lunch with my mentor, Pat Williams, the co-founder of the NBA's Orlando Magic. I'd written a letter to him when I was running TicketAdvantage, to ask if he would be an advisor to my fledgling company. He graciously agreed to do so, probably thinking I would never call on him for any help. Boy, was he wrong! One afternoon at lunch, when we were discussing my future, Pat said, "Why

MY OBJECTIVE WAS TO HELP BUSINESS PROFESSIONALS AND SPEAKERS CREATE, PUBLISH, AND MARKET BOOKS THAT WOULD HELP THEM TO GROW THEIR BUSINESSES.

• •

don't you start a publishing company for business professionals?" At that time, Pat was one of the top motivational speakers in America, speaking 120 times a year, crisscrossing the country to give inspiring presentations and talks to Fortune 500 companies, school districts and universities, and professional associations.

While that idea had never occurred to me, it made sense as soon as he said it. When I was in high school, I had spent two summers as an intern at a large publishing company, working with the marketing, sales, editorial, and design departments. They even sent me over to the warehouse for a couple of days where I picked, packed, and shipped books and sent them out to customers. I'd thought that I would hate publishing—but I loved it. I'd always been a reader, especially of business books, and this exposure to the book business fascinated me. But was it enough on which to build a startup? Pat convinced me that my two summers working for a publishing company as an intern had taught me more than what

99.9 percent of people knew about the business. And when I expressed my self-doubt, he told me, "Whether you think you can or you can't, you're right."

That conversation was the genesis of my startup, Advantage Media Group, one of the companies I lead today. My objective was to help business professionals and speakers create, publish, and market books that would help them to grow their businesses. At the beginning, it was just myself and a part-timer. I took a tabletop trade show display to the National Speakers Association convention in Atlanta, and I walked out of that three-day conference with thirteen signed contracts and thirteen deposit checks. Luckily, no one asked if they could speak with a satisfied author . . . because there weren't any yet! I've always believed in the idea of "sell it, then build it." I came back to Charleston and realized, "Holy smokes. I've got to figure out how to create books, and quick." I soon found a freelance designer and a freelance editor and began assembling books. I was twenty-three years old.

"WHETHER YOU THINK YOU CAN OR YOU CAN'T, YOU'RE RIGHT."

In 2016, Advantage partnered with Forbes, the biggest name in business media, to create For-

Here I am with Steve Forbes at the Authority Summit in January 2018.

besBooks. Suffice it to say, the company and I have grown and matured tremendously since day 1. Today, Advantage|ForbesBooks helps busy CEOs, entrepreneurs, and professionals become THE authority in their field. We've pioneered Authority Marketing®, in which we position, promote, and market our Members and their businesses as thought leaders and experts through books, content, publicity, speaking, lead generation, and omnipresence. More than two thousand Advantage|ForbesBooks Members hail from forty US states and twenty-three countries. All of our growth has been accomplished without investors or venture capital.

But it wasn't all smooth sailing; I learned on the fly, and there were plenty of mistakes in my trial-and-error phase. I had never run a business before, except for my little start-up in college, and everything was happening very quickly. The culture I created in the first five years was passable, but not many of the people working at Advantage then would have put their hands up if asked whether they were excited to come to work on Monday.

Unfortunately, there aren't many classes or books that teach how to be a great CEO. Most early experience is about making mistakes and then being smart enough to learn from them. My first seven years as a CEO is what I call "The Lost Seven." I was winging it. I didn't know how to hire people, I didn't know how to grow people, and I didn't know how to retain people. I knew enough about sales and marketing to get by, but I wasn't smart enough to realize that the only way the business could grow was if I was growing people. I thought, "Well, I'm the best salesman, so I need to be doing the selling"—but if the CEO is the only salesperson in the company, then that company is never going to grow to be very big. There were so many simple principles like that that I didn't even consider.

That first seven years we grew to $1.5 million in sales, but we were barely squeaking by. I had maxed out our line of credit. We had two or three weeks of cash on hand, and if things didn't go well or customers

I WASN'T SMART ENOUGH TO REALIZE THAT THE ONLY WAY THE BUSINESS COULD GROW WAS IF I WAS GROWING PEOPLE.

. . . .

weren't paying on time, I was looking at insolvency. I had to take out a home equity loan against my small condo so we could make payroll on three separate occasions, because we didn't have any cash reserves. Around 2012, I realized that it was time to decide whether I wanted to be an amateur or a real professional, to decide whether I was going to play small ball or move up to the big leagues.

It all goes back to the nature of entrepreneurship; every great entrepreneur and CEO that I know is somebody who relishes the challenge of growth. They don't want to stagnate. They want to push themselves and they want to push their organization. My problem was that I was getting comfortable; not rich, clearly, but even though I was barely getting by, there was a level of complacency setting in that was at odds with what I knew real entrepreneurship entails. It was time to get serious about growth and catch up on the education I'd missed in college. I actively connected with mentors; I picked up my reading and delved into every business book I could get my hands on.

AROUND 2012, I REALIZED THAT IT WAS TIME TO DECIDE WHETHER I WANTED TO BE AN AMATEUR OR A REAL PROFESSIONAL, TO DECIDE WHETHER I WAS GOING TO PLAY SMALL BALL OR MOVE UP TO THE BIG LEAGUES.

. . . .

And it paid off. Since 2012, we've grown from 30 percent to 100 percent annually. (In five years since, we've grown by a factor of 20x, after having used the company's first seven years just to get to that $1.5 million.) But not all of the changes can be measured in dollars; many of them were cultural and not so easy to quantify. Our culture at the beginning was passable; if you walked in the door, it wasn't obvious that the culture was toxic. Had you dug a bit deeper, you would probably have found that many people weren't very happy. People didn't feel like they knew what was going on, and because of that, they felt trapped and suspicious. Had you asked them if they looked forward to Mondays, most of them would have told you that they looked forward to Fridays. I knew that, and it was a real disappointment to me, but I also knew that I was the only person who could change the status quo. I made it my business to right the ship and over the last six years, we've achieved success in creating a culture where people actually look forward to Monday. Does this mean that every moment of every day 100 percent of the people will raise their hand and say, "I can hardly wait for Monday!" No, but I can say with confidence that the large majority of our team feels engaged, empowered, and professionally fulfilled. They know what's going on, they embrace the daily challenges; they're excited about the direction, goals, and purpose of the company, and believe that they're making a difference by being a part of it.

Where are you, and where's your company, on the scale of engagement? You may be at the same place I was in 2012, and you might not even know it. But if you could hear what your employees really thought about their work and their boss, you might be mortified.

WHAT DOES A GREAT WORK CULTURE LOOK LIKE?

Let's consider an Olympic rowing team, with eight athletes on the racing shell. These athletes are in impeccable physical condition with mental conditioning to match. When the first pair of oars hit the water, the other seven pairs are hitting the water in perfect synchronicity. They're all rowing the same direction and with the same amount of force, and watching them cut through the water is a thing of beauty in its precision and speed.

Your employee team needs to function like that rowing team—but in most companies, anywhere from 30 to 50 percent of a workforce is *disengaged*. If they're passively disengaged, that means they're not willing to put their oars in the water. If four members of your eight-person team aren't pulling their weight, then the remaining four people are forced to do all the work. And what if two of those are actively disengaged—they're so resentful of their jobs and you that they're intentionally undermining the company's goals and rowing in the opposite direction?

As CEO, you're the coxswain, tasked with motivating your team as well as steering a straight course. You're trying to get that boat across the finish line as expeditiously as possible. But you've got two who aren't

AS CEO, YOU'RE THE COXSWAIN, TASKED WITH MOTIVATING YOUR TEAM AS WELL AS STEERING A STRAIGHT COURSE. YOU'RE TRYING TO GET THAT BOAT ACROSS THE FINISH LINE AS EXPEDITIOUSLY AS POSSIBLE.

· ·

rowing at all and two who are rowing in the opposite direction! Your chances of winning are nil. That's why creating a functional, dynamic culture in your workplace is everything. If you can create an environment that your people are excited to come to on Monday morning, you're going to see a big difference in the speed with which you can accomplish your goals.

CHAPTER 1

GETTING IT RIGHT

ING GHT

"IF YOU DON'T DO IT EXCELLENTLY, DON'T DO IT AT ALL. BECAUSE IF IT'S NOT EXCELLENT, IT WON'T BE PROFITABLE OR FUN, AND IF YOU'RE NOT IN BUSINESS FOR FUN OR PROFIT, WHAT THE HELL ARE YOU DOING THERE?"

—ROBERT TOWNSEND

GETTING IT RIGHT

THERE ARE TWO PHRASES

every entrepreneur and CEO has heard, and they make my spine shiver every time I hear them.

The first phrase is "Thank Goodness it's Friday." What does TGIF really mean? Allow me to translate: *I hate my job and can hardly wait to get the hell out of here for the weekend!* I suppose you could put a Pollyanna spin on it and say, "People love their family time and look forward to that," but now you're just being gullible. TGIF signals a BIG problem in the workplace today; people don't like what they do and they want to get away from it. How disappointing is it that people live for two days per week and barely tolerate the other five?

The second phrase is "Hump Day." This one means the workweek is finally halfway finished; you're finally over the hump. Why is it that we're so excited that half the week is finally over? Because we don't like our jobs.

It's easy to poke fun at these attitudes, but it's disappointing when you consider how ubiquitous they are, and what that says about how people feel about their professional lives. Surveys consistently show that regardless of what kind of company you lead, whether large or small, for-profit or nonprofit, about 50 percent of your employees are not happy in their jobs.[1] That's a depressing statistic, no matter how you look at it. What kind of progress is a company going to make when half of its workers are at best disengaged, and at worst, actively sabotaging it? For an entrepreneur and CEO who wants to grow, that's a very frustrating place to be.

When people aren't happy at work, if you're lucky, you'll lose them. If you're unlucky, they'll stick around. Most unhappy and disengaged employees will mentally quit; they just won't have the decency to tell you, and they'll keep collecting a paycheck every two weeks. They'll do just enough to get by. They'll make everybody else miserable and they'll become a cancer inside of your organization. If your employees are happy, that gives you a powerful competitive advantage in the marketplace.

WHEN PEOPLE AREN'T HAPPY AT WORK, IF YOU'RE LUCKY, YOU'LL LOSE THEM. IF YOU'RE UNLUCKY, THEY'LL STICK AROUND.

· ·

1   Susan Adams, "Most Americans Are Unhappy At Work," *Forbes*, last modified June 20, 2014,https://www.forbes.com/sites/susanadams/2014/06/20/most-americans-are-unhappy-at-work/#34587b50341a.

Not only is it going to help you attract and recruit high-caliber people, but it also means that your happy employees are going to take care of your customers.

Unhappy workers create unhappy customers, and unhappy customers don't pay their bills on time. They request refunds and aggressively spread the word about their experiences, bad-mouthing your company. If your customers are happy, they will propel your profitable growth. Happy customers pay on time. They're typically willing to pay more, and they become advocates and ambassadors, telling anybody who will listen about you and your business. Thus, that happiness, which starts at the top, can have a tremendous trickle-down effect. It's not easy, and certainly there's not an exact formula—but it is possible.

Need another reason to improve the culture in your workplace? Here's one: if your workplace isn't happy, you will lose employees, which is costly. Most people don't calculate how much it costs to lose someone: let's say you have a copywriter who works on your marketing team. He makes $50,000 a year, and he asks for a $5,000 raise; you decide that even though he's doing good work, his request is unreasonable. You're not going to give him the raise, so he decides to go elsewhere. You're probably thinking, "I can go out and hire somebody else for $50,000, so I'm going to save the company $5,000." But have you added in what your time is worth? How many hours is it going to take for you to recruit, hire, and then ultimately onboard that new person? From my own experience, I can tell you that it will take at least a hundred hours. Another thing: let's say the copywriter who left because you wouldn't give him a $5,000 raise had been with your organization for two and a half years. What is his two and a half years of institutional knowledge worth? A lot. In fact, here's what the data says: the cost to replace someone can be anywhere from one to four times that person's annual salary.[2] That means that while you were patting yourself on the back for saving $5,000, the truth is it probably cost you somewhere between $50,000 and $200,000 to let that guy walk out the door.

IF YOU CAN CREATE A COMPANY WHERE PEOPLE SAY TGIM, INSTEAD OF TGIF, THEN THE COMPETITIVE ADVANTAGE THAT YOU HAVE AND YOUR ABILITY TO QUICKLY GROW IS EXPONENTIAL.

2   Christina Merhar, "Employee Retention-The Real Cost of Losing an Employee," *ZaneBenefits*, last modified February 4, 2016, https://www.zanebenefits.com/blog/bid/312123/employee-retention-the-real-cost-of-losing-an-employee.

This is why it's so important to create an environment where your people look forward to Monday. If you can create a company where people say TGIM, instead of TGIF, then the competitive advantage that you have and your ability to quickly grow is exponential.

Let's talk for a moment about the word *culture*, a word that makes many in business wince. When people hear the word *culture* around business theory, they immediately think of ping-pong tables, Beer Fridays, or Bring Your Dog to Work Day. Most assume that *culture* means giving people a lot of free bells and whistles, perks that probably distract them from the work they're supposed to be doing. Everybody thinks that you have to spend a ton of money. When somebody says the word *culture*, the first reaction from a CFO is, "How much is this going to cost?"

I don't believe that's what *culture* means. To me, culture is recruiting, hiring, and training the best people while creating an environment in which they are equipped to do their jobs exceptionally well. Empower them, recognize them, reward them, and give them room to grow; that's what great culture is. Great culture is creating an atmosphere that supports A-players, because the one thing that everybody would rather have than free beer on Friday or ping-pong tables is A-player colleagues who are really good at what they do. It's frustrating when your coworkers are idiots, but when your coworkers are all-stars, it makes work a lot easier and a lot more fun. It's easy to focus on perks, and the reason it's easy to focus on those bells and whistles is that it lets you avoid focusing on the deeper and more challenging issues. The deeper issues are what's at stake if you want your people to say, "Thank Goodness it's Monday."

EMPOWER THEM, RECOGNIZE THEM, REWARD THEM, AND GIVE THEM ROOM TO GROW; THAT'S WHAT GREAT CULTURE IS.

To solve the problem, you really have to roll up your sleeves and systematically attack it, creating an environment that breeds greatness one step at a time. At this point, you're probably excited and thinking, "Great! I have the opportunity to really make my business something special," and the truth is, you do. It starts with you; the company that you have today is 100 percent a reflection of you, so if you're unhappy with the business you have today, then you should be unhappy with yourself. If the culture is toxic, then you need to accept that the toxicity is flowing from the top down. Remember, water flows downhill!

Let's start there.

CHAPTER 2

A GREAT
COMPAN
WITH YO

STARTS

U

"FOR THE PAST THIRTY-THREE YEARS, I HAVE LOOKED IN THE MIRROR EVERY MORNING AND ASKED MYSELF: 'IF TODAY WERE THE LAST DAY OF MY LIFE, WOULD I WANT TO DO WHAT I AM ABOUT TO DO TODAY?'AND WHENEVER THE ANSWER HAS BEEN 'NO' FOR TOO MANY DAYS IN A ROW, I KNOW I NEED TO CHANGE SOMETHING."

—STEVE JOBS

A GREAT COMPANY STARTS WITH YOU

MY IDEAS ABOUT WHAT IT MEANS

to be a leader have evolved quite a bit—which relates back to where we left off: the business you have today is a direct representation of you. If you're unhappy with the business, it's you. If you're happy with the business, it's you. Bad business is a consequence of bad leadership. A great business is a result of great leadership. The good news is that the power to fix this lies in your hands.

My first seven years in business—my Lost Seven—definitely had an attitude of "What the hell do you want from me? I'm giving you a job. I'm giving you an opportunity. Why aren't you grateful?" That attitude isn't unusual among business owners. I learned from first-hand experience that this attitude is decidedly unhelpful, because it does nothing to move the culture or environment of the company forward. It really is a 50/50 proposition, just like any relationship. Both sides must contribute.

Someone always has to make the first move and provide the impetus for forward motion. In your business, the instigator of progress MUST be you. If you're not happy with where things are, don't point the finger at other people. Instead, take a look in the mirror. When you walk around your office on a day-to-day basis, what mood are you projecting to the people who work with you? It matters much more than you might think. It took me a long time to accept the idea that the company's mood could rise and fall with mine. That was true when we had ten employees; it's still true, although we've grown to the point where I could easily spend a day in our headquarters and not see three-fourths of the people in the company on any given day. When we're all in one big room together,

IN YOUR BUSINESS, THE INSTIGATOR OF PROGRESS MUST BE YOU. IF YOU'RE NOT HAPPY WITH WHERE THINGS ARE, DON'T POINT THE FINGER AT OTHER PEOPLE. INSTEAD, TAKE A LOOK IN THE MIRROR.

it's evident to me that the mood of the room rises and falls with how I'm coming across. YES, that is the effect that all leaders and CEOs have, whether you like it or not. I'm a pretty serious guy; I've lightened up a lot in the last five years, but at the start, my characteristic "let's-get-down-to-business" vibe was perceived negatively, which created an unhappy atmosphere for the entire company. When that became clear to me (and several people were helpful enough to point it out), I decided to make an effort to ensure that when I'm interacting and engaging with people, I'm projecting a hopeful, optimistic, positive attitude. It's also important that I be excited about things, because if I'm not excited, how can I expect others to get excited? I have to lead by example.

It's not always easy for people; there are many introverted entrepreneurs and CEOs who start companies, and that's fine. Extroverts don't have a birthright claim to starting businesses. But if you're not an extrovert, if you're not a naturally bubbly, outgoing person, then you must acknowledge that and make a conscious effort to recalibrate your personal presentation. Remember that your facial expressions, body language, choice of words, and even your tone of voice are observed by EVERY employee you interact with. Make sure that you project positivity.

HOW DO I KNOW IF I'M
GETTING IT RIGHT?

How do you know if you've got it right or wrong? Here are some things to look for:

→ If you hear people use the phrases Hump Day or TGIF, then you've probably got it wrong.

→ If you look out your office door at 5:01 p.m. and see empty chairs still spinning because the people who were in them jumped up and ran out of the building so damn quick, then you've probably got it wrong.

→ If you've ever felt like there's an "us versus them" or a "management versus labor" feeling, then you've probably got it wrong.

→ If you, the leader, aren't happy, then I can assure you that you've got it wrong. Life is too short to be in a job or career that doesn't make you happy. I know many entrepreneurs and CEOs who feel as if they're chained like prisoners to their businesses. The truth is that it is nobody's fault but theirs. If you're not happy, then your people probably aren't either.

→ If there's an office grapevine; if there's political maneuvering or backstabbing, that's a good sign you've probably got it wrong.

→ If you're afraid to ask for feedback because of what you're going to hear—not a good sign. A lot of people purposely avoid asking for feedback because they know what they're going to hear is bad, and they just don't want to deal with it.

→ If your immediate assumption when you bring a new idea or a proposal to the table is that the feedback is going to be negative, that could be a sign that you've probably got it wrong.

It's important to remember that it's human nature to focus on what's broken and needs to be fixed, so when you're beginning to have the conversations about "What do I need to do to create a great environment in my business?" people will want to talk about the problems and what needs fixing. It's your job as the leader to steer the conversation toward more positive and productive channels: "Great. Thank you for that feedback. Just out of curiosity, what would you say we're doing right? What's going well?" Why? If you don't focus your questioning and your request for feedback on the positive as well as the negative, then you're subliminally communicating you agree that, "Yeah, everything is broken." It's up to you to provide a balanced view. If you ask people what's going right and they can't think of anything or they have blank stares on their faces—that could mean you've got a problem.

Back in my Lost Seven, it drove me nuts when my fellow team members didn't work as hard as I did, or at least that was the story I told myself in my head! Why weren't people as invested in and as passionate about the business as I was? It took me a while (you would think this would be obvious!) to figure out part of it

IT DROVE ME NUTS WHEN MY FELLOW TEAM MEMBERS DIDN'T WORK AS HARD AS I DID, OR AT LEAST THAT WAS THE STORY I TOLD MYSELF IN MY HEAD!

· ·

was that they didn't own the company—I did. This was my baby, my creation; they came onboard to help it grow, but it wasn't their baby. You may have a nanny to look after your child, and even though that nanny may take great care of the child, it's unlikely the nanny's going to love the child as much as you, the parent. The other thing I realized is that if the team members in my organization wanted to be entrepreneurs, then they'd be out doing it on their own. Not everybody has the gumption and comfort with uncertainty that an entrepreneur does, and that's good. That's not a value judgment, it's just a statement of fact. If there weren't people in the world who wanted to work for businesses rather than start their own, then we'd have no real businesses.

You, as the leader, must get over wanting everyone to be as committed as you are. As many wonderful people as there are at Apple, I can promise that when Steve Jobs was alive, there wasn't anybody who obsessed day in and day out as much about Apple as Jobs did.

There were people who worked very hard and there were people who gave their passion and their souls to their job, but not to the same degree that Jobs did. If you engage and empower your people and give them opportunities to grow, they'll be happy and they'll do phenomenal work—and that will be good enough.

If you want to create an environment where people look forward to Monday, then you have to believe yourself. You have to be the cheerleader. You have to be the merchant of hope. You have to be the one repeating the message "We're doing exciting work together, and we are making great progress and we are having a big impact."

Another important thing you must do is hire great people (we will talk more about this in Chapter 8), because a team of A-players creates an environment that breeds greatness. If you're working with idiots and you're the one who always picks up their slack, then you're going to be unhappy with your job. If your colleagues and coworkers are smart, competent, and able to do their jobs well, then everyone's in sync and happy.

Your criteria as the leader in making hiring decisions is basing your choice on the greater good, which means that when you hire someone, you have to ask, "Is this person going to collectively raise the quality of talent in the company? Is this person going to collectively raise the quality of the department?" If

**WHEN YOU KEEP
THE PERSON WHO
IS FUNCTIONALLY
COMPETENT, BUT
CULTURALLY A DISASTER,
YOU'RE SUBLIMINALLY
COMMUNICATING TO
EVERYBODY THAT THE
BEHAVIOR IS OKAY.**

the answer is no, then don't hire that person. They may be incredibly skilled at what they do, but if they're bringing baggage of negativity or narcissism with them, then they're going to be toxic to the culture you're trying to build. Don't fall in love with a resume when you should be assessing the person as a whole.

I have certainly made this mistake in the past and it's tough to live with and tough to fix. You know what I am talking about; the person you hired who is technically proficient but is a jerk nobody likes. You know you've fallen into this trap when you hear yourself or others saying things like, "Well, they're a little hard to deal with, but they're really good at what they do," or, "I feel like I'm walking on eggshells whenever I'm around them," or, "Boy, we've got to treat him with kid gloves." These are all phrases people use when they have somebody that's functionally performing very well, but who culturally is a real problem. As the leader, you feel handcuffed; "Boy, I don't want to let this guy go because he's bringing in a million dollars in sales to our business every year. But the truth is everybody in the company hates him."

Here's what you're doing: when you keep the person who is functionally competent, but culturally a disaster, you're subliminally communicating to everybody that the behavior is okay. You're telling them: "We'll put up with this jerk and his abusive/manipulative personality, because he's good for the bottom line." It's critical that you not be lured into the fear of losing them because they're proficiently sound. You've got to make the hard decision to let them go, because culturally and attitudinally, if they can't get onboard, then they will work against everything that you're trying to do.

When planning, remember the ecosystem that exists. Here's how it works: there are five key stakeholders in any for-profit organization. You've got employees, which we at Advantage call team members. You've got customers or clients; at Advantage, these are our Members. You've got shareholders or investors, which could include the founder of the business, partners, or actual investors who have put money into the business. The fourth piece of the ecosystem are vendors and suppliers. These are the companies you do business

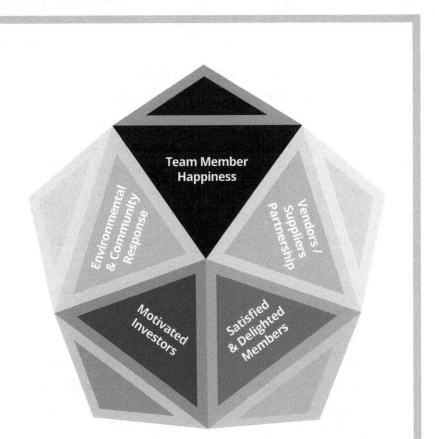

Advantage. **Ecosystem**

with so that you can ultimately do business with your customer. The fifth is the community (or communities) in which your business is located. I conceptualized this ecosystem in the interests of raising awareness around the idea that, long term, in order for an ecosystem to thrive, its components must be in balance. If things are out of balance, long term, one of those components is going to wither and die.

So, how does that happen? Let's say, as an example, you need one customer service rep for every ten customers, but you decide, "We could really save some money if we could just automate some of this and cut our customer service reps down by half." So now, instead of a 1:10 ratio, it's 1:20. You're going to save the company money, which benefits the shareholders temporarily, but by cutting down on service, you're going to infuriate and frustrate your customers, and that means they're not going to spend as much. They're going to drag their feet paying their bills. They're not going to enthusiastically refer you to other people. When that happens, revenues start to drop. At the same time that you're shortchanging the customer, you're also shortchanging your employees, because now your employees have to deal with angry customers all day.

If you work for a company where your job is focused on interacting with customers, would you be happy on Friday afternoon if you had interacted all week with people who are happy to a be a customer of your company? On the other hand, how would you feel by Friday if you'd spent the whole week reactively dealing with people who are upset and dislike your company? When you decide to double the number of accounts assigned to each customer service representative, one sector of your ecosystem might see temporary

WHEN YOU DECIDE TO DOUBLE THE NUMBER OF ACCOUNTS ASSIGNED TO EACH CUSTOMER SERVICE REPRESENTATIVE, ONE SECTOR OF YOUR ECOSYSTEM MIGHT SEE TEMPORARY BENEFITS, BUT IF IT'S AT THE EXPENSE OF ANOTHER PART OF THE ECOSYSTEM, THEN ULTIMATELY EVERYONE WILL SUFFER.

. . . .

benefits, but if it's at the expense of another part of the ecosystem, then ultimately everyone will suffer.

This chapter began with "a great company starts with you" and ends that way, because in order to create an environment that people really look forward to being a part of, there must be more to it than just money. There must be earned success and there must be fulfillment. It's your job to inspire them, to create a core purpose for your business that has meaning, and that's where the next chapter will begin.

CHAPTER 3

THE
FOUNDA
NOBLE

"NO MISSION, NO MARGIN."

—PATTI MOORE

THE FOUNDATION: A NOBLE PURPOSE

IF YOU WANT TO HAVE AN ENVIRONMENT

where people look forward to coming in on Monday, then the people in your organization must feel like they are on a noble mission (or purpose); part of an endeavor that will make a difference and have a positive impact on people's lives. Do people come to work because they need money to pay the bills, to put food on their table? Yes, but what sustains people and what ultimately elevates people to their highest level of work is the sense of worth they get by being connected in a meaningful way to the work they're doing.

There are a lot of different kinds of companies in the world. Some have very noble purposes: curing cancer, saving lives. If your company makes tobacco products or sells sugary beverages, it might be harder to see the nobility of the purpose. If your company paints houses or manufactures ball bearings, creating a noble mission around the work is going to be harder, but is still very possible. If you peel back enough layers of the onion, just about every business can find an exciting and noble purpose people who work there can be proud of.

You must remember it has to be about more than just making money. If not, it will be tough to attract and retain the best people, because if it's only about money, there will always be another company that can offer more. If your company isn't about more than just the paycheck that you provide, your people will jump ship at the first better offer they get. This is why a noble purpose is vital.

TALK ABOUT OUR DEMOGRAPHIC AND THEIR NEED FOR US

YOU MUST REMEMBER IT HAS TO BE ABOUT MORE THAN JUST MAKING MONEY. IF NOT, IT WILL BE TOUGH TO ATTRACT AND RETAIN THE BEST PEOPLE, BECAUSE IF IT'S ONLY ABOUT MONEY, THERE WILL ALWAYS BE ANOTHER COMPANY THAT CAN OFFER MORE.

WHAT IS THE NOBLE PURPOSE
OF YOUR BUSINESS?

What impact does your company have on the world? I'm going to use Advantage as an example. Our noble purpose, also called our *core purpose*, is to **Grow Entre-preneurs and Businesses to Benefit All Mankind**. By helping our Members become the Authority in their field, more than two thousand Advantage and ForbesBooks Members now walk the earth sharing their books, giving motivating and uplifting speeches, appearing on TV and radio, and sharing their stories, passion, and knowledge with others, which grows their business and benefits everyone associated with that business.

That's our noble purpose, and it's easy to get people excited about it. When you hear the phrase, "The right book in the right hands can change a person's life forever," most people will buy into that. And whether you're an editor, a designer, a sales rep, or an accountant, you play a vital role in helping the company fulfill its mission of helping more Members share their story, so we can help more people learn and grow, and grow businesses at the same time.

We publish financial and money management books, health and wellness books, motivational books, marketing books, and leadership books. And whether that book teaches the reader how to improve their financial position and get out of debt, inspires the

GROWING

ENTREPRENEURS

&

BUSINESSES

TO

BENEFIT ALL MANKIND

reader to finally lose those last thirty pounds for good and reclaim their health, or helps the reader become a better leader and improve the lives of the people who work for him—regardless of the topic, the right book in the right person's hands can literally change that person's life forever.

That's our unique purpose, but every entrepreneur and CEO can find his or her own with a little soul searching. What impact can your company have on the world? What positive effects do the products or services your company offer have on customers? Once you figure that out, it's the CEO's responsibility to articulate and communicate that noble purpose, not just once, but forever. If you're constantly talking about your noble purpose, then you're going to attract people who are interested in it. If some people don't feel called to your purpose, that's okay, because those are people you don't want working for your company anyway. The people who are excited about it will become your "band of

IF YOU'RE CONSTANTLY TALKING ABOUT YOUR NOBLE PURPOSE, THEN YOU'RE GOING TO ATTRACT PEOPLE WHO ARE INTERESTED IN IT. IF SOME PEOPLE DON'T FEEL CALLED TO YOUR PURPOSE, THAT'S OKAY, BECAUSE THOSE ARE PEOPLE YOU DON'T WANT WORKING FOR YOUR COMPANY ANYWAY.

brothers," inspired and committed to doing whatever it takes to help the company achieve its purpose.

EXAMPLES FOR ILLUSTRATION: THE NOBLE PURPOSE

Getting that noble purpose right is the most important thing you can do for your business, and is a primary focus for you as its leader. Steve Jobs was on a crusade to make technology both accessible and beautiful, to create the intersection between technology and design where home computers would be simple and elegant, both aesthetically and functionally. Had he not been passionately committed to that mission, and able to inspire others with his passion, it's hard for me to believe that Apple could have created the Mac, iPhone, iPad, or the iPod. That kind of excellence requires total company commitment.

Most people don't particularly enjoy flying, because the service generally stinks. The people working on the airplane don't exactly make you feel like an honored guest; the subliminal message is, "Get in. Put your bag up, sit down, and shut up." There was a man many years ago who thought flying should be fun, cost-effective, and accessible to more people. His name was Herb Kelleher, and the company he co-founded is Southwest Airlines. Southwest's stock ticker symbol is LUV, and Herb Kelleher said, "The reason our stock

IT'S YOUR RESPONSIBILITY TO CRAFT, ARTICULATE, AND COMMUNICATE YOUR NOBLE PURPOSE, AND IF YOUR PURPOSE IS JUST TO MAKE MONEY, THEN YOU'RE GOING TO LOSE THE REALLY GOOD PEOPLE.

. . . .

symbol is LUV is because it represents the love we have for our customers." Now, *that* is a purpose: democratizing the skies and loving your customers so more people can fly. That is a noble purpose that many people can get excited about.

I don't know what noble purpose American or United have, but I can't think it is loving their customers and democratizing air travel. So, if you're a pilot or a flight attendant, and you're one of the very best, what company would you rather be a part of, Southwest or United? Chances are you're going to be more attracted to the noble purpose of a company like Southwest over its competitors.

If you've ever flown Southwest, you know the flight attendants are fun. They rap and rhyme when they do the safety demonstration. They wear shorts and polo shirts. They're lighthearted people, and the culture and purpose attracts those kinds of people. This is why the purpose must come from the CEO. It's your responsibility to craft, articulate, and communicate your noble purpose, and if your purpose is simply to make money, you're going to lose the really good people. Most people aren't wired to be money-hungry at all costs.

You can't fake purpose. People will see through it, and people will see through you. You must find people who are really into what they do. You must find people who really love, live, and breathe what your company does. At Advantage, our tagline is "The Business Growth Company." Through our Authority Institute and our book publishing business, we position, promote, and market our Members as the authorities, experts, and leaders in their field. This helps our Members grow their business. If you're not *for* entrepreneurs, then I can't imagine why you would want to be a part of our team. If you don't believe a country with an abundance of growing businesses ultimately benefits all, just as an incoming tide lifts all boats, then I can't imagine why you would want to be a part of our company.

For most businesses, especially startup or entrepreneurial businesses, the purpose is largely an outpouring of the heart of the leader. For example, the Walt Disney Company's purpose is to put smiles on children's faces, to create a world of happiness for children. Nobody believed in that mission more than Walt Disney himself.

In fact, had it not been for Walt's strong insistence on that mission permeating the entire organization, The Walt Disney Company as we know it today would probably not exist in the capacity that it does.

When the founder of a company leaves, oftentimes the company will slide. They forget their true purpose. They start chasing squirrels. They make it all about money, and the company loses its way. It wasn't until Steve Jobs returned in the early 2000s that Apple really got its groove back, because they had a leader who believed in the purpose more than anybody else in the entire company.

HOW DO YOU CREATE THAT NOBLE PURPOSE? THIS IS WHERE YOU AS THE LEADER HAVE TO THINK DEEPLY; "WHY IS IT THAT I DO WHAT I DO?

How do you create that noble purpose? This is where you as the leader have to think deeply; "Why is it that I do what I do? Why did I start this company in the first place?" It's not just to make money. Yes, money is a byproduct, and everybody needs money to survive, yet most leaders will tell you there are places they could go and make more money. It's not the money that keeps them there, it's the purpose. The purpose of the company is not something that should be created by committee, it's ultimately something that has to be crafted by the leader.

I've always believed deeply in personal and professional development. I'll be honest, when I initially created the business, I saw it as an opportunity to both serve people and to grow something that would make money. Since I founded Advantage, I've read a number of powerful books that helped clarify the importance of purpose for a business. But it wasn't until my fifth year that I realized how critical it was to get this right. I crafted our purpose over a period of many weeks: "What is it that we do? We market, position, and promote our Members as the Authority in their field. But no, no, no, that's not really what we do. Why do people listen to experts and authorities in the first place? Well, to learn. Okay. Now we're getting somewhere. People listen or read to learn about a topic, and if it's a business or professional or a self-improvement matter, they are listening or reading to learn and grow." I liked where this was going.

It was an iterative process; it didn't happen on Day 1—although, if you could figure out the purpose before you started the business, you'd be better off. If I'd had a strong noble purpose when I started, then I probably could have avoided my "Lost Seven" years.

How important is the purpose when it comes to capturing your peoples' hearts and minds, and rallying them to work together toward a common goal? When you look at people who enter the armed services in America, especially those who are infantrymen, they

Is it just about service?

enter knowing they may lose their lives. Yet they join, knowing that they are a part of something that's bigger than themselves, and that something they're "for" is the United States of America. What does America really stand for? It stands for freedom. The brave men and women who knowingly put themselves in harm's way are doing so because they are invested in the purpose, and the purpose is to preserve and protect freedom. When you look at people who rallied around Martin Luther King Jr. and the civil rights movement, it was about something far bigger than just any one person; it was about equality. Why is it that Martin Luther King Jr. was able to rally millions of people around an idea? It's because it wasn't about him; it was about a noble purpose, and that noble purpose was that—regardless of color, creed or ethnicity—all people should be treated equally.

So, while I'm not making the claim that your business or my business's purpose is as noble as freedom or equality, if you can create a purpose for your business that's even a tenth as powerful as either of those, you will get people invested in helping fulfill a noble purpose that could span their entire careers.

GET PEOPLE
INVESTED
IN HELPING
FULFILL
A NOBLE
PURPOSE THAT
COULD SPAN
THEIR ENTIRE
CAREERS.

CHAPTER 4

CRAFTI

YOUR CO

VALUES

"TELL ME WHAT YOU VALUE AND I CAN PAINT A PICTURE OF YOUR LIFE."

—ANONYMOUS

CRAFTING YOUR CORE VALUES

NOW THAT YOUR CORE PURPOSE

is clear to you, it's time to talk about core values, values that will support the purpose you're invested in. Let's start by defining our terms. Everyone has a set of unique core values that guide them. I might not subscribe to the values you hold dear, but that doesn't mean either of us is wrong.

Families have core values. Many companies have core values—but, unfortunately, they're too often relegated to a plaque in the lobby, where nobody looks at them. I'll bet if you walked into the office of any manager at a company and asked, "What are the core values of this company?" few, if any, could tell you, including the CEO. Meaningful values must be impactful, and they must reflect the heart and soul of the company. Core values will make decisions easier, because this set of guiding principles serves as a sort of moral compass to which you can refer when making tough decisions. Without core values, every decision you make is agonizingly difficult because there is no set of guiding principles to follow.

CORE VALUES WILL MAKE DECISIONS EASIER, BECAUSE THIS SET OF GUIDING PRINCIPLES SERVES AS A SORT OF MORAL COMPASS TO WHICH YOU CAN REFER WHEN MAKING TOUGH DECISIONS.

• •

The CEO shouldn't bring the core values to team members as if he were Moses coming down from the mountain with stone tablets. I know, because that's what I did the first time! When I started Advantage, I personally crafted all of the company's core values. They weren't the company's values, they were MY values. I had to learn the hard way that if I wanted to get people invested in the core values, it was far better to ask for their input and then help make the values their own, because people gladly adhere to values that are theirs. The second time around, I engaged everybody in the company over a three-month period to help us craft the core values that the people of Advantage would live by. There were only fourteen people in the company at the time, but we had everybody come up with a list of core values, and then we wrote them on a big white board. There

The Advantage Core Values.

was a lot of overlap, with people saying similar, if not identical, things. Any core value that two or more people suggested, we'd put a little check mark next to it. There were five or six that a lot of people shared, and those were the values we zeroed in on.

CORE
VALUES

BUILD
THE ADVANTAGE FAMILY

TAKE
INITIATIVE AND
BE RESOURCEFUL

If you run a company with 5,000 team members, it's going to be very hard to get everyone's input. If you have a smaller company, whether it's twenty-five people or fifty people or even a hundred people, it's much easier. Regardless of size, you need to find a way to let your people be heard in the crafting of these values, because when they have no input in them, they cross their arms and say, "I'm not going to follow these dumb values," and that's the one thing you want to avoid. When you create your values as a group, you get buy-in, and when you have buy-in, it's easier for you to accomplish your agenda as the leader of the business.

Your core values will inform every corporate choice you make. They serve as a benchmark for hiring, they set the standard for promotions, and they're one of the most valuable guides for when to let people go. Everyone needs to be held accountable to the company's core values. For example, one of ours is to *create an environment that breeds greatness*. Advantage is a place of energy, enthusiasm, and fun. Our team is comprised only of A-players who collaborate and honor teamwork. We

YOUR CORE VALUES WILL INFORM EVERY CORPORATE CHOICE YOU MAKE. THEY SERVE AS A BENCHMARK FOR HIRING, THEY SET THE STANDARD FOR PROMOTIONS, AND THEY'RE ONE OF THE MOST VALUABLE GUIDES FOR WHEN TO LET PEOPLE GO

believe that positivity breeds productivity, and with a great attitude and an open mind, anything is possible. What would be a deviation from that value? How about bad-mouthing colleagues or talking negatively about your coworkers? How about spreading rumors? How about playing the game of office politics and trying to plot against co-workers? In most businesses, managers look the other way. If that stuff's going on at Advantage, it's a perfect opportunity to say, "Hey, Bill, I saw what you just did. Help me understand. One of our core values is to create an environment that breeds greatness. You know that and I know that, and what you just did is in direct conflict to that value. Why'd you do it?" That becomes an opportunity for you to engage and have a substantive conversation. And here's the thing; if people aren't willing to live by the values, then they need to find another organization that has values they are willing to live by.

A lot of people hire and fire based on technical performance. There are a lot of people who are proficient at their jobs, technically speaking, but who have lousy attitudes, and quite frankly can wreak havoc on your company culture. When a leader knowingly allows that damage to happen, the leader is subliminally communicating to everyone in the company that that behavior is okay. By doing so, you created a precedent and set an example that will be tempting for others to follow.

USING CORE VALUES IN HIRING

Hiring is really tough, because everybody's on their best behavior. Geoffrey Smart, author of *Who*, the best book on hiring I've ever read, said "a resume is a document in which everyone's accomplishments are embellished and their failures are omitted." That's also true of the interview process; you only see people's good sides. So, how can you hire effectively when everybody's on his or her best behavior? One way is values-based interviewing. Advertise those values on your website, in your marketing literature, and in your job postings. When we interview candidates, we specifically ask them, "What was it that attracted you to Advantage? Tell us a little bit more about our values and how they may have spoken to you." Then we listen for truth or B.S. We want people to articulate which of Advantage's values resonated with them personally, because again, it all goes back to the noble purpose. If you don't value entrepreneurs and businesses growing, then why do you want to be at a company that promotes that as its core purpose? You're not going to be happy. You're not going to be successful, and long term, everybody's going to lose. The core values are a way for us to identify who's with us.

If people make it to a more advanced stage in our recruiting process, three different people will interview the candidate based upon the five core values we have, and the candidates have to share examples of things they have done in their career or in their personal life applying values of the same or similar nature. If they have a hard time sharing that, they're probably not aligned with our values, and Advantage probably isn't the company for them. If the question strikes home, you can see the enthusiasm in their face; you can hear it in their voice, in their language, and in their answers. Those are the ones who make the final cut.

Values really are at the heart of everything. If you create strong values, hire, fire, and promote according to those values, and truly build an organization that lives the values each and every day, then success becomes much closer.

VALUES REALLY ARE AT THE HEART OF EVERYTHING. IF YOU CREATE STRONG VALUES, HIRE, FIRE, AND PROMOTE ACCORDING TO THOSE VALUES, AND TRULY BUILD AN ORGANIZATION THAT LIVES THE VALUES EACH AND EVERY DAY, THEN SUCCESS BECOMES MUCH CLOSER.

CHAPTER 5

WHAT
YOUR

S
BHAG?

"I BELIEVE THAT THIS NATION
SHOULD COMMIT ITSELF TO
ACHIEVING THE GOAL, BEFORE
THIS DECADE IS OUT, OF
LANDING A MAN ON THE MOON
AND RETURNING HIM SAFELY
TO THE EARTH. NO SINGLE
SPACE PROJECT IN THIS PERIOD
WILL BE MORE IMPRESSIVE TO
MANKIND, OR MORE IMPORTANT
FOR THE LONG-RANGE
EXPLORATION OF SPACE."

—PRESIDENT JOHN F. KENNEDY

WHAT'S YOUR BHAG?

HAVE YOU GOT A BHAG?

BHAG stands for Big Hairy Audacious Goal, a term that was coined by the legendary business author and speaker Jim Collins, who many of you probably know as the author of *Good to Great, Built to Last, How the Mighty Fail,* and *Great by Choice.* The concept of the Big Hairy Audacious Goal is: what will your company do to impact the world in a big way? What is your big idea, and how big is it? Big enough that people, on hearing it, would tell you, "That's impossible. There's no way that you can do that"? Because if your BHAG elicits responses like, "Oh, yeah, that's attainable, we can reach that," then it's probably not big, hairy, or audacious enough.

For a lot of companies, a BHAG is a ten-, fifteen-, or twenty-year goal. Most people in an organization don't have the ability to see ten, fifteen, or twenty years down the road, but entrepreneurs and CEOs have traits that most people do not, one of which is vision. There's a famous story about Walt Disney: Walt was touring a group of bank officers through an orange grove in Anaheim, CA, the site that would ultimately become Disneyland. Walt had a vision and he could literally see where Cinderella's Castle was going to be, where Tomorrowland was going to be, where the Main Street USA was going to be. He was pointing at a grove of orange trees, saying, "That's where the castle's going to be." The bankers, who he was hoping would finance his vision, couldn't see it the way he did, of course. Entrepreneurs, CEOs, and leaders must realize that we can see the future like a high-definition Technicolor movie, while all anyone else sees is a picture in grainy black and white, if they can see it at all. The same holds true for your BHAG. When most people walk down the street, they look down at their feet and the sidewalk in front of them. Leaders look up and forward to where they want to go.

That's why I personally believe the way to get people excited about a Big Hairy Audacious Goal is to make the accomplishment of that goal a little bit more short term, say five years away. For most people, five years from now is a really long time, but they can fathom it, whereas fifteen or twenty or twenty-five years from now seems beyond most people's ability to imagine. I like a more compact Big Hairy Audacious Goal in the five- to seven-year range. Most people in the organization, if they're committed to and excited by that BHAG, can stay with the organization long enough to help achieve it. And if they really feel like they can be a part of achieving it, in my opinion, then they're going to work harder and more diligently to help the organization reach it.

In December 2013, I unveiled Advantage's five-year BHAG. At the end of 2013, we were working with roughly sixty-five active Members, helping them grow

their business. Our BHAG is that by December 31, 2018, Advantage will be working with a thousand active Members. That means that we'll be fifteen times the size of what we were at the end of 2013.

The first response most people gave me was, "Wow." The second thing they said was, "How are we going to do that? I don't think we can." Your job as a leader is to push people to accomplish things that they didn't think they could. This is why Michael Jordan had a coach. This is why LeBron James has a coach. This is why every famous athlete has a coach; as good as they are, there is a coach out there who can push them to do more.

GOOD LEADERS PUSH THEIR PEOPLE TO ACCOMPLISH MORE. NOT JUST BECAUSE THEY WANT MORE PRODUCTIVITY; THAT'S A HAPPY BYPRODUCT. THE BIGGER REASON YOU WANT YOUR LEADERS AND MANAGERS TO PUSH YOUR PEOPLE TO DO MORE IS YOU WANT TO GROW YOUR PEOPLE.

That's the job in business as well. Good leaders push their people to accomplish more. Not just because they want more productivity; that's a happy byproduct. The bigger reason you want your leaders and managers to push your people to do more is you want to grow your people. If you create a company where everyone is growing, you become a company of giants. A BHAG can truly be a galvanizing force that not only gets people excited, but also gives your leadership team the opportunity to coach and grow people to accomplish more than they ever would have thought possible. I like to say that a BHAG, in many ways, is really the definition of how your company's going to change the world and what the world and the company will look like when it happens.

If your BHAG initially elicits a negative or uncertain response, don't take it personally. That's coming from FUD: fear, uncertainty, and doubt, from an inability to connect the dots to see how it will all come together to actually happen. It's coming from a reluctance to change. It's human nature to resist change; we like knowing what to expect. When there's no predictability, it makes us uneasy because predictability is what allows us to survive. If you went to bed every night wondering whether or not the sun would rise in the morning, you'd have a pretty rough night. Because we're confident the sun will rise, we don't lose any sleep over it. The change required to accomplish a BHAG means the predictability that people have day in and day out is going to fluctuate—and that immediately triggers fear.

What got us to where we are is not necessarily what will get us to where we want to go. To do that, we must change, we must do things differently. That means we're going to have to expand and hire more people. We're probably going to need to let some of our more tenured people go if they're not able to adapt, change, and grow with the company. We're going to have to rethink and retool our marketing plan. We're going to have to adjust our finance plan, perhaps raise outside capital.

When I rolled out that five-year plan to grow from sixty-five active Members to a thousand active Members, with the exception of a couple of key leaders, there was nobody in the room who actually thought it was possible. And that's okay. That doesn't mean people don't care about the company. It just means I was asking people to stretch so far their first reaction was resistance. You should expect that to happen. You must slowly but surely show progress and inch by inch move closer toward that goal. Eventually, you will have converts. People will begin to believe. Your Big Hairy Audacious Goal is an elephant, and there's only one way to eat an elephant—one bite at a time.

Speaking of elephants, the big elephant in the room is this: you're going to have to modify and adjust your plans. You're going to learn information that will cause you to correct your course. When you're looking at a five- to seven-year plan, you have anywhere from 1,800 to 2,500 days to accomplish this plan. Take it one day at a time.

Since launching our Road to 1000, we've made a lot of progress. As I write this, we've just wrapped up our company-wide quarterly Business Plan Review. Every ninety days, we invite team members to anonymously submit questions. I stand at the front of the room and I answer everyone's questions. One of the questions was, "I 1000 percent believe in the Road to 1000 and I know that we as a company will get there. My question is, with all of the changes and with all of the new people hired, I'm worried about how I fit into the plan." To me, a question like that is a great sign, but it also tells me that we need to make sure that we're communicating and helping people understand how they're a part of it. When you hear somebody say, "I 1000 percent believe in this BHAG," that's a good sign, and that can be contagious. When you have core believers, they begin to pollenate and spread that message among their colleagues and, with time, you have more and more converts and believers to the BHAG.

Don't confuse your BHAG with your purpose. Our core purpose at Advantage is to Grow Entrepreneurs and Businesses to Benefit All Mankind. Our BHAG is a thousand active Members by December 31, 2018. How do those tie together? If we help a thousand Members Grow Themselves and Their Businesses, as opposed to just sixty-five Members, then the positive impact that we make on the world is now multiplied by a factor of fifteen.

My strong suggestion is that you don't make your BHAG a revenue or financial goal. If you want great people committing to your goal, then it must be about the mission and the sense of fulfillment they get by being a part of that mission. Those are the people who'll be eager to see Monday roll around, because they're motivated to help the company achieve a meaningful milestone.

In 1960 when John F. Kennedy was elected president of the United States, he set a Big Hairy Audacious Goal in his inaugural address: to send a man to the moon before the decade was out. When he said those words, we were far from being able to make that a reality. Many people thought, "There's no way that's going to happen. This president is crazy." But before the decade ended, America sent a man to the moon, the first country to do so. And those immortal words by Neil Armstrong, "One small step for man, one giant step for mankind," are etched in many people's memories. I'd argue that had President Kennedy not challenged his country with the Big Hairy Audacious

Goal, it would not have happened. That's the power that a BHAG can have in your organization.[1]

In the book *The Progress Principle*, authors Teresa Amabile and Steven Kramer make the case that the most important thing in someone's professional career—the thing that keeps them happy, engaged, and looking forward to Monday—is feeling and seeing progress on a regular basis. That means personal progress, departmental progress, and company progress. Who wants to be a part of a company that is stagnant or, even worse, contracting or declining? No A-player does. All boats rise with the tide, but when the tide is going out all boats fall, as well.

To achieve a BHAG, sometimes you have to fall behind before you can speed ahead. The key to get people to buy in to the BHAG is to be transparent about those setbacks. If you had a poor quarter in performance in moving toward your BHAG, then you have to come out and say, "We didn't meet the mark. We did not meet the expectations we had set for ourselves, which means we've got to work harder." Don't sugarcoat it, and certainly don't sweep it under the rug and ignore it. People are looking to you, and your transparency in sharing where things stand, good or bad. It is one of the most important things in getting your team members to buy into your BHAG.

---

[1]   "BHAG – Big Hairy Audacious Goal," *Jim Collins*, http://www.jimcollins.com/article_topics/articles/BHAG.html.

TO ACHIEVE A BHAG, SOMETIMES YOU HAVE TO FALL BEHIND BEFORE YOU CAN SPEED AHEAD. THE KEY TO GET PEOPLE TO BUY IN TO THE BHAG IS TO BE TRANSPARENT ABOUT THOSE SETBACKS.

. . . .

At Advantage, we have a gong on the first floor of our office where our Member Development team is based. Every time we welcome a new Member into the Advantage family, the Member Development team member who brought on the new Member rings the gong, and you can hear it throughout the entire building. Everybody claps and cheers, and jumps up to see who just rang the gong! We also have scoreboards set up throughout our offices, flat screen TVs with constantly rotating slides that show the progress that we're making toward our goals on the Road to 1000. Every time a book is published, Nate Best, a member of our editorial team, plays a song on the company trombone. Everyone throughout the entire building can hear that, too. It creates positive chatter, "What book just got published?!" You have to celebrate the milestones toward your BHAG.

ACCOMPLISHING YOUR BHAG IS SO FAR AWAY IT'S HARD FOR MOST PEOPLE TO COMPREHEND. YOU HAVE TO REWARD PEOPLE FOR ACHIEVING MILESTONES ALONG THE WAY IN MUCH SMALLER INCREMENTS.

• •

Accomplishing your BHAG is so far away it's hard for most people to comprehend. If someone were to say to you, "If you work really hard for me, in seven years I'm going to give you a large bonus," chances are it wouldn't do anything to motivate you because the payoff is too distant. You have to reward people for achieving milestones along the way in much smaller increments; in calendar quarters, monthly, and, in some cases, weekly or even daily.

THE PAINTED PICTURE

Earlier in this book I talked about the importance of having a BHAG; that big, hairy, audacious goal you're working toward. Generally in a business, the CEO or entrepreneur has a clear picture of what that future looks like. It's all there in their imagination, and in bright Technicolor to boot! But for most people who are working in the business, the company's future is in grainy black and white. If you want to create an environment that makes your people say, "I'm looking forward to Monday," those people have to share your vision of where the company's going. It's easy to be enthusiastic about a bright future you can see – but when what's ahead is cloudy and opaque, it's a lot harder to get excited about it. So how do you paint the vivid, living picture of your company's future that will energize your team?

A practice that I started a number of years ago was something called The Painted Picture, an idea pioneered by entrepreneur Brian Scudamore of 1-800-GOT-JUNK, which is a master document I update on a quarterly basis. The Painted Picture is a three- to four-page document that explains in vivid detail what our company will look like when we accomplish our BHAG. Reading The Painted Picture out loud every quarter helps our team members to see what I see, and to get a real fix on what the future will look like when we achieve our goals together.

The more that people in your organization can share in your vision of the bright future in store, the more excited they'll be about working together towards achieving those goals. When what you're moving toward is clear and defined, it makes it easy to look forward to Mondays.

Remember the words of Ronald Reagan, our 40th president: "Leadership is giving credit when things go right and taking the blame when things go wrong." If you want to get every single person in your company excited and galvanized toward your BHAG, then all of the credit along the way for successes must go to other people, and all of the blame for missteps and failures ultimately must fall on you and your senior leaders. You must shower praise consistently.

READING THE PAINTED PICTURE OUT LOUD EVERY QUARTER HELPS OUR TEAM MEMBERS TO SEE WHAT I SEE, AND TO GET A REAL FIX ON WHAT THE FUTURE WILL LOOK LIKE WHEN WE ACHIEVE OUR GOALS TOGETHER.

DON'T FORGET TO HAVE FUN

Want your people to look forward to Mondays? You've got to make work fun. We do that with contests, games, and giveaways, because I believe the more we can "game-ify" the work our people do, the more interactive, the more collaborative, and the more fun it is. At Advantage, we have something called *quarterly themes,* and every quarter we have a company-wide contest. If we hit our goal, then there's a big prize, but even if we fall short of a goal, there's still a celebration. It doesn't include the big prize, but we still have reason to celebrate. That idea came from Advantage Member Verne Harnish, who wrote a terrific book that's really the model for business growth, *Scaling Up.*

Rallying people around a shared, purpose-driven goal creates the kind of unit cohesion that makes going to work a positive experience, and will have team members looking forward to Mondays.

One of the ways we've done this has helped reinforce a central theme in our business—our Big, Hairy, Audacious Goal we call The Road to 1000. That's why we named our theme for calendar year 2018 *Fast and Furious,* after the famous movie franchise that's all about muscle cars and speed. But how could we make the theme resonate for our team? Since Road to a 1000 uses the analogy of a road and driving to get to a destination, that brought us to the idea, "Wouldn't it be fun to give away a brand-new car to one deserving Advantage team member?"

Here's what we decided to do: Every week in 2018, we let team members nominate each other for going above and beyond in helping the company live the Fast and Furious theme. From among those nominees, the senior leadership team picks a weekly winner. That winner will receive the keys to a 2018 Ford Mustang convertible for the week. We cover the gas and a car wash; they get to drive a fun and flashy car. We plan to do this for about fifty weeks until the annual holiday party, where the names of all of those who won a week with the Mustang are put into a hopper. Five of those names will be drawn, and each of those five given a key. One of those five keys will start the Mustang—and the person who gets the key that works, drives the car home for life.

The 2018 Fast and Furious Mustang giveaway is an inspired way to reward performance, reinforce a key theme in our business, and make it fun all at the same time. If working harder toward the company goals earned you a shot at a new Mustang, wouldn't you look forward to coming to work on Mondays?

Our "Mustang Wall", depicting all of our weekly winners.
Inset: An Advantage team member poses with the
Mustang after being selected as a weekly winner.

Advantage Quarterly Theme Posters.

Advantage Quarterly Theme Posters.

CHAPTER 6

HAVE A PL

AND COM

THE PLAN

"HAVE A PLAN, WORK THE PLAN,
AND ALWAYS KNOW THE STATUS
OF THE PLAN AND THE AREAS
THAT NEED SPECIAL ATTENTION."

—ALAN MULALLY

HAVE A PLAN AND COMMUNICATE THE PLAN

IF YOU WANT TO CREATE A WORLD-

class organization where people look forward to Monday, you've got to have a strategic plan for your business—and you've got to share it with your team members. Too often, businesses trying to grow either don't have a comprehensive plan in place, or they fail to communicate that plan to the rest of the company.

Typically, an executive team goes through the strategic planning process annually and comes out with an actionable plan, but in most cases, they never share that plan with the rest of the people in the company. If they do communicate it, too often they're just doling out bits and pieces of it on a "need to know" basis. That makes it difficult for those left out of the planning process to understand how their efforts help the company get to where it wants to go, because they can't see their place in the big picture.

THE COSTS OF CONCEALMENT

Why are so many of those in leadership hesitant to share their plans with their frontline people? Unfortunately, a lot of people have internalized the idea that getting and holding power or influence in an organization requires withholding information from others, and keeping them in the dark about plans. The thinking is that if I have a lot of information and my colleagues don't, it gives me leverage and increases my value. It's a perverse idea, and it erodes trust.

But when you have a plan that you communicate with your team, and when you're open, honest, and transparent about what the business is trying to do and how each person plays a role in affecting it, then slowly but surely, trust can be built.

Trust is one of those things that can and will rise and fall; it's not as if you arrive at some point where it's etched in stone and will endure forever. If you look at trust in government, trust in business, or trust in organized religion, confidence in any of these institutions can rise or fall depending on the events of the day, week, month, or year. In the same way, the level of trust that frontline team members have in senior leadership can rise and fall too. As leaders, we need to constantly be looking for ways to establish and reinforce trust, to put deposits into that "trust bank" so they're there for us when we need them.

Let's face it: sooner or later, every company is going to screw up. When that happens, it's going to require a withdrawal in that trust bank. The objective is to have enough deposits in the trust bank that, when there is a withdrawal, it doesn't cause you to bounce a check. That's why having and communicating your strategic plan is so critical to your success—that willingness to share is a big step toward building trust and, with it, rallying your people around your common goals.

I believe that if you can create a compelling plan that's easy to understand, and you can communicate that plan to every single person in the company, it creates alignment in a business—and alignment produces results. Look at a gold medal Olympic rowing team for a lesson in what alignment can accomplish: everyone's clear on their role, the whole crew is pulling in the same direction, and all of them are contributing a similar level of vigor and precision into their work. There's no ambiguity around what's needed to move the boat forward; nobody's just looking around with their oar out of the water, wondering what to do. They all share the same objective and are clear on how to get there.

In business, what happens when you don't share your strategic plan with your team members? Some of them won't have their paddles in the water. Others who aren't clear on what they're expected to do may row vigorously in the wrong direction. Still others, resentful at being left in the dark, may row lethargically, effectively sabotaging the efforts of those teammates who are really trying. Even those who are rowing in the right direction may have trouble keeping the pace that leadership's trying to set.

If you've got ambitious goals for your organization, you've got to have everyone on your team pulling powerfully in the same direction with comparable force and vigor. That alignment comes from a shared understanding of goals and what it will take to reach them—and the only way to accomplish that clarity is through communication. When people understand not only what's required of them but also *why*, they're able to pull together more effectively, and are far more likely to be emotionally invested in the effort. Everyone wants to be part of a winning team, but it's up to you as their leader to create that necessary cohesion.

IF YOU'VE GOT AMBITIOUS GOALS FOR YOUR ORGANIZATION, YOU'VE GOT TO HAVE EVERYONE ON YOUR TEAM PULLING POWERFULLY IN THE SAME DIRECTION WITH COMPARABLE FORCE AND VIGOR. THAT ALIGNMENT COMES FROM A SHARED UNDERSTANDING OF GOALS AND WHAT IT WILL TAKE TO REACH THEM.

KEEP IT SIMPLE AND
STAY THE COURSE

I opened this chapter with a quote from one of my CEO "crushes," Alan Mulally, who was the CEO of Boeing Commercial Airplanes from 2001 to 2006 and then Ford Motor Company from 2006 to 2014. During one of the most challenging periods in the history of the US automotive industry, Ford was the only American automaker that didn't require a federal bailout to stay in business. Why? I would argue that Mulally's ability to turn Ford around hinged on the compelling strategic plan he created for the company. He simplified the language of that plan so that everyone in the company—all four hundred thousand people, from the C-suite to the factory worker on the production line—could understand it. He communicated the plan relentlessly and worked on it religiously, making sure that there were only minimal deviations.

Sticking with your plan and staying on course is more of a challenge if you're among those who tend to turn in the prevailing wind like a weather vane. Particularly in smaller companies led by an entrepreneurial founder, when a new a new idea, opportunity, or bright shiny object swings into view, the entrepreneur goes chasing after it, and the strategic plan is abandoned. That means that the business has to change direction too, which can be tremendously demoralizing to the people in the organization. Just when they're getting a sense of momentum and can see progress toward a goal, the goalposts are moved and they've got to refocus.

If you're trying to produce a working environment that makes your people look forward to Mondays, creating and sharing an easy-to-understand plan is a powerful step in the right direction. At Advantage, we've built that kind of a plan. Within our plan, there are four quadrants, titled: (1) Publish to Prosper, (2) Business Growth Partner, (3) Best Place to Work, and (4) Fund the Future. In creating these, we kept the idea of simplicity front and center, because we wanted the overall plan to be easily understood.

In order for us to achieve the kind of growth we want, we recognized there were four main areas we needed to focus on. At our core, the foundation and the origins of our business are in book publishing, and what brings most of our Members to us initially is the desire to write and publish a book. That's why "Publish to Prosper" is a key strategic plank in our plan. Within that quadrant, we have a number of sub-points of ambitions and aims that we need to address going forward to streamline our publishing process to make it quicker, easier, and more cost-effective. We know that if we can hit those goals, it will make us even more attractive as a publishing partner. If we're more attractive, we can arguably draw more people through the writing/publishing front door, from where they can ultimately move into other areas of membership available in our company.

What goods or services do you sell? Clearly, whatever your product is, the impetus is on you to figure out where your front door is; i.e., how do most people come to see you as a provider of goods or services and what's their most likely point of entry? Identifying and enhancing that "front door," whatever it is for your business, should be a key piece of your strategic plan.

The second pillar in our plan is titled "Business Growth Partner," which goes back to our "why": Why do our Members want to write and publish a book? They want to write and publish a book to establish themselves as the authority in their respective fields, to be recognized as thought leaders, and to share their expertise with others. Why do people want to share what they know with others? Typically it's because they want to have an impact. The more they can share what they know, the more people they can reach; the more people they reach, the more they can be of service to the world, and the more they're of service to the world, the more likely it is that others will be moved to come to them and say, "I want to do business with your company."

The fundamental belief at Advantage is that if you stop chasing money and concentrate instead on being of service to others, the money will follow. This pillar of our plan is about moving forward strategically in ways that will help us to be of greater service to our

> **THE FUNDAMENTAL BELIEF AT ADVANTAGE IS THAT IF YOU STOP CHASING MONEY AND CONCENTRATE INSTEAD ON BEING OF SERVICE TO OTHERS, THE MONEY WILL FOLLOW.**

Members, and to be better business growth partners. That involves taking into account what our members need to succeed in their efforts and, where appropriate, adding new lines of service or new products to help them achieve that success.

For you reading this book, I would encourage you to go through a similar process; if you peel back the onion's layers and ask why it is that a customer is coming to do business with you and look at that on a holistic basis, you'll probably find there are other products and services that your customers would love to buy from you.

The third quadrant of our four-quadrant strategic plan is "Best Place to Work." The concept here is quite simple: At the end of the day, our team members are our greatest asset. Our belief at Advantage is that if we focus first on team member happiness—which means creating an environment in which team members can be successful, engaged, and fulfilled in the work they do—those happy team members will take great care of our Members. If our Members are well taken care of and are successful with their work, profitable growth will be the result.

The problem in business is that most companies put the shareholders' interests first. Once the shareholders are taken care of, they look after the customers. After the customers are taken care of, then and only then do they consider the employees. If that's how you view the hierarchy, I think you've got it backward. Take care of the team member, i.e. the employee, first. The employee will take care of the customers. The customers will take care of profitable growth, and that will make your shareholders happy. For us, being the best place to work is all about creating an environment that attracts the best and brightest, because the company that has the best and brightest will deliver the best products and services with the fewest mistakes. When everyone wants to work for your company, the A-players come to you. That gives you leverage in hiring, and allows you to be that much more selective about who you invite in. It's like being the best looking girl or the most handsome guy in town. They can be pretty darn selective about whom they choose to go out with, and they don't have to settle for second best. Neither do we.

The fourth quadrant in our strategic plan is entitled "Fund the Future." Cash is oxygen to a business, as critical to keeping an enterprise alive as oxygen is to keeping you alive. If a business doesn't have enough cash, it can't pay team members, it can't pay vendors, and it can't pay rent. What does that mean? It means you have to lay people off, and you have to downsize. Eventually, if you still don't have enough cash, you either file for bankruptcy or you close down the business for good. We are a fast-growing entrepreneurial company, and cash is necessary to fund our growth. "Fund the Future" is all about managing the business in an economically responsible way so that we have the resources to fund our growth plan.

SHOW ME YOUR CARD!

Those four quadrants are the bedrock of our Road to 1,000 strategic plan. Every important decision that we make as a company is based on that plan. All of the chess moves we make as a business tie back to the plan, whether it's a new position we're creating, or an acquisition we're considering. When we make a move, every single person in the company can look at the Road to 1,000 four-quadrant strategic plan and say, "Oh, I see why we did that."

How certain am I that our team members are clear on our plan and united around our mission? I've made it easy for them. Every Advantage team member has a card the size of a regular credit card in his or her wallet, and printed on one side of the card is our Road to 1,000 plan. On the flip side is our core purpose, our core values, and the eleven practices and principles of "Working Together." This was another nifty idea that I got from Alan Mulally.

My goal in sharing our plan and our values this way was to make it so simple to understand that it can literally fit on a wallet-sized card. Every single Advantage team member gets one of these and carries it. At company meetings, I will give out money to people who have the card in their wallet. Yes, I'm bribing them—I'm not going to lie. But it's important to me that they have the card with them for a couple of reasons. Number one, whenever the business seems complex, whenever they're overwhelmed, whenever they feel like they can't understand how all of the pieces fit together, all they have to do is pull out their wallet card, review the plan, and see how it all comes together.

The second thing I'm trying to subtly communicate with this card is how much importance we place on the idea of alignment across the company. If everyone's clear on the plan, that helps create alignment. If every decision we make is aligned with the plan, then that creates a sense of calm and helps eliminate worry or misunderstanding. If everyone literally has the plan in their pockets and can internalize it, they can see how the work that they do day in and day out moves the company toward achieving its goals.

Is your strategic plan compelling? Exciting? Is it clear enough that all of your team members can understand it? Is it simple enough to print on a wallet card, so that everyone who works in your business can carry it with them?

I jokingly tell the people in our company, "The next time you're out to dinner with friends, ask them about their company's strategic plan—and be prepared to hear a lot of 'uh's and 'um's because they probably don't have a clue." Our people invest over forty hours of their week with us, almost certainly more time than they have with their own families. If they're going to invest that kind of time with us, I think they have a right to know why we're doing what we're doing—and I think they should want to understand it, because it will help them see how what they do contributes to the bigger picture.

That's how we keep our team rowing in the same direction.

The Advantage business plan on a wallet-sized card.
Every team member carries one with them at all times.

CHAPTER 7

"THERE ARE THREE KINDS OF PEOPLE IN THE WORLD TODAY. THERE ARE 'WELL POISONERS' WHO DISCOURAGE YOU AND STOMP ON YOUR CREATIVITY AND TELL YOU WHAT YOU CAN'T DO. THERE ARE 'LAWN MOWERS,' PEOPLE WHO ARE WELL INTENTIONED, BUT SELF-ABSORBED; THEY TEND TO THEIR OWN NEEDS, MOW THEIR OWN LAWNS, AND NEVER LEAVE THEIR YARDS TO HELP ANOTHER PERSON. FINALLY, THERE ARE 'LIFE ENRICHERS'—PEOPLE WHO REACH OUT TO ENRICH THE LIVES OF OTHERS, TO LIFT THEM UP AND INSPIRE THEM. WE NEED TO BE LIFE ENRICHERS AND WE NEED TO SURROUND OURSELVES WITH LIFE ENRICHERS."

—WALT DISNEY

TALKING THE TALK

WHEN YOU'RE TRYING TO CREATE

an environment that breeds greatness, one in which your people look forward to Monday, communication with them and the words you use are vital. What you say and how you say it communicates your priorities as a leader, and it communicates the priorities of the organization. To get people excited about being a part of your company, you must communicate passionately and eloquently. You must also express priorities that are beneficial to your team members. If the priorities of the company are in conflict with the interests and needs of your team, then they're not going to get excited. You have to check

WHAT YOU SAY AND HOW YOU SAY IT COMMUNICATES YOUR PRIORITIES AS A LEADER, AND IT COMMUNICATES THE PRIORITIES OF THE ORGANIZATION.

the words that you and your leadership team employ. You have to ask yourself, "Is the language I use empowering or disempowering?"

For example, consider the impact of the phrase *leadership team* as opposed to *management team*. It's my belief that people don't want to be managed. People want to be led, people want to be nurtured, they want to be coached, and they want to be pushed up, but they don't want to be managed. When I hear the word *managing*, the first thing that comes to my mind is *meddling*. We all know the term *micro-managing*; I don't think there's anyone who'd say being called a micromanager is a compliment. So, when you hear the word *manage*, what do you think? Here's what I hear: your team members are drones who can't be trusted, who aren't able to make smart decisions themselves, so you as the manager must carefully keep your eye on them to make sure they don't screw things up. That's what *manage* communicates subliminally to me.

On the other hand, when I hear the word *leader*, I think of Abraham Lincoln. He led America through its deepest and darkest hours. I think of Dr. Martin Luther King Jr. I think of Steve Jobs or Herb Kelleher. I think of visionaries who pushed people up, inspiring them to do and accomplish more than they thought possible. Simply using the words *leadership team* as opposed to *management team* communicates something positive and important about how you see your business.

Another word I absolutely despise is *employee*, because it implies to me, "I pay you to work here; shut up, be grateful that you have a job, do what you're told, and don't bring any baggage in with you." The word *employee* to me is transactional. In order for you as the leader to have fun in business, the people that are in business with you need to be having fun too. To me, the word *employee* doesn't signify that. It signifies a transaction.

A much better descriptor is *team member*. As a kid, I played sports and I'm a huge sports fan to this day. I believe that when the team wins, everybody wins. When the Chicago Bulls won a game, it wasn't just Michael Jordan who had the satisfaction of victory, it was every single person on the team. As you try to build a culture in which people look forward to Monday, and as you build a culture that's marching toward your BHAG, everybody on the team must be able to win together. If they don't feel like they can win, they're going to either leave or, worse, be miserable and quit working, but not have the decency to tell you! They'll keep collecting a bi-weekly paycheck. You need people who are engaged. *Team member* communicates that we're all in this together, and that our success is intertwined.

Another term that makes me cringe is *HR—yuck*. Whenever you say "You need to go talk to HR," the image people have in their mind is some person who doesn't want to be there but helps you deal with the bureaucracy and the B.S. associated with being an employee in a company that exists solely to make a profit. I much prefer the phrase *team member success* department. The whole point of HR is to make sure that everyone is successful, so calling the department team member success communicates the mission more accurately than *HR* or *human resources*, which communicates that every person in your company is simply a resource to be managed from 9 a.m.–5 p.m. Here's the thing: if you don't like humans, if you'd prefer to not to deal with humans, then starting a company that depends upon them is probably not a good idea.

HERE'S HOW I DEFINE LEADERSHIP: ACCOMPLISHING RESULTS THROUGH PEOPLE. IF YOU WANT TO BUILD AN ORGANIZATION OF ANY SUBSTANCE AND SIZE, REGARDLESS OF INDUSTRY, THEN YOU'LL LIKELY NEED A LOT OF TEAM MEMBERS WORKING ALONGSIDE YOU.

. . . .

I learned this the hard way, because when I first started Advantage, I would have rather watched paint dry than deal with the issues and challenges my people were bringing me. My attitude was, "I'm smart enough to figure this out on my own. Why can't you?" I cringe thinking about what an immature reaction that was at the time. Your job as a leader and as a CEO is to lead people. Here's how I define leadership: *accomplishing results through people.* If you want to build an organization of any substance and size, regardless of industry, then you'll likely need a lot of team members working alongside you. Growing a business means growing head count. And if you hate dealing with people, then you'd better find somebody that likes it, and completely remove yourself—or consider a different occupation.

Growing a business is one of life's ultimate challenges in size and significance, and requires coaching people to achieve higher levels of performance in which they will grow too. How you communicate impacts how you are heard. At Advantage, we have an exercise we go through together as a company every six months called "unifying our message." Everybody has an 8.5" x 11" laminated flash card to keep on or near their desk that has the exact language that we as a company use to describe things. For instance, our Members make an *investment* in working with us. It's not a cost and it's not an expense. When our Members introduce us to someone else, in most companies they'd say, "Oh, would you give me a referral?" We like to use the word *introduction*. *Referral* says to me, "Would you introduce me to your friend because I want to make money by selling them something?" Whereas, with "You mentioned to me that you had a friend who was a business owner that was interested in doing a book. Not sure if we could be of any help to her, but I'd certainly appreciate an introduction," you're saying the same thing, but it sounds completely different. Words matter.

I DON'T LIKE POLICIES. GUIDELINES, ON THE OTHER HAND, EMPOWER YOUR PEOPLE TO USE THEIR BEST JUDGMENT TO RESOLVE SITUATIONS.

I prefer the term *guidelines* over *policies*. Have you ever been to the front desk at a hotel, or the ticketing desk of the airline, and you ask for something and they say, "Our policy is we don't do that"? Well, here's what that language communicates to me: when you say "our policy," that means, "We don't really give a damn about you as a human being and we're too lazy to adapt to unique individual situations that face our customers, so the answer is no." A guideline, on the

UNIFYING OUR MESSAGE

WHO ADVANTAGE | FORBESBOOKS IS FOR

Entrepreneurs, Business Leaders, and Professionals who care about growing their business.
Our mission is to help our Members share their Stories, Passion, and Knowledge to help others Learn & Grow.

WHAT ADVANTAGE | FORBESBOOKS OFFERS

Advantage is The Business Growth Company™.
We help our Members and their business become the authority in their field.

PUBLISHING	MARKETING	SPEAKING
Talk Your Book®	Authority Marketing System™	ForbesSpeakers
Talk Your Book® Ghostwriting	Branding & Omnipresence	
Launch Your Book®	Content Marketing	
	PR & Media	
	Speaking	
	Lead Generation	
	Referral Marketing	
	Events	

HOW ADVANTAGE BACKS IT UP

MEMBER PROMISE

1. Build a brand that establishes you and your business as an authority in your field
2. Craft and implement a plan to grow your business
3. Provide an Easy, Fun, and Prosperous membership experience

The "Unifying Our Message" one-sheeter each team member keeps at their desk.
Reverse side on opposite page.

other hand, leaves room for a team member to make an exception for a customer when there's an extenuating or special circumstance.

Spirit Airlines has a policy that most airlines have: all sales are final. Once you purchase a ticket, if you change your mind, get sick and can't make the trip, it doesn't matter, because all sales are final. Many airlines will let you change your flight for an absurd "change

CORE VALUES

CREATE AN ENVIRONMENT THAT BREEDS GREATNESS
Advantage|ForbesBooks is a place of energy, enthusiasm, and fun. Our team is comprised only of "A" players who collaborate and honor teamwork. We believe that positivity breeds productivity and with a great attitude and an open mind, anything is possible.

MAKE A DIFFERENCE
Our Team Members are driven by the "why" of what we do. The right content in the right person's hands at the right time can change the world forever. We believe in sharing Stories, Passion, and Knowledge to guide and help others Learn & Grow.

BUILD THE ADVANTAGE FAMILY
We consider every Team Member, Member, and supplier an extended member of our family. These men and women are the reason we exist. We strive to serve with excellence so we may build and maintain lifetime relationships that contribute to their success.

TAKE INITIATIVE AND BE RESOURCEFUL
At our core is an entrepreneurial spirit that drives our team to constantly innovate. We rely on creative individuals who aren't afraid to defy the status quo, experiment with new ideas and introduce bold solutions to the challenges of our time.

COMMIT TO LIFELONG LEARNING
We seek to uncover and promote the leader in every one of us by encouraging all Team Members to follow a path of personal and professional development. We believe that increased **knowledge, experiences, and skills leads to a more fulfilled life.**

7 STANDARDS OF SERVICE

S SUPPORT
provide solutions

E EDUCATE
share knowledge

R RESPECT
embrace diversity

V VALIDATE
build confidence

I INSPIRE
deliver possibilities

C CULTIVATE
create community

E ENGAGE
initiate conversation

OUR LANGUAGE

MEMBERS Not authors, not clients, not customers. Always capitalize the M in Members in all written communication.

TEAM MEMBERS **Not employees. Not staff. Always capitalize the T and M in Team Members in all written** communication.

INVESTMENT Not cost. Not fee. Members are making an investment in growing their business that will provide substantial returns.

ELEVATOR SPEECH Advantage|ForbesBooks is the Business Growth Company™. We help busy entrepreneurs, **business leaders, and professionals become an authority in their field.**

fee," which is oftentimes more expensive than the actual ticket you purchased. Spirit doesn't even let you do that. All sales are final, and if you don't make the flight, tough. There was a recent story about a Vietnam veteran who'd planned a trip, but was subsequently diagnosed with terminal cancer. When he called the airline and shared his story, they said, "Well, sorry, but all sales are final." This created a melee of media outrage on every major network. And to make matters worse, the idiot CEO defiantly went on all of these news shows and reiterated that the company's policy is they don't refund ticket purchases, period, even if you are a Vietnam veteran who is terminally ill. Spirit Airlines probably received $5 million worth of negative publicity because they wouldn't refund that gentleman $147. That's why I don't like policies. Guidelines, on the other hand, empower your people to use their best judgment to resolve situations.

Now, let's drill down a bit further. You're trying to recruit A-players. If you have a team of A-players, people are going to be performing and hitting their goals. And you know what happens when people in companies hit their goals? People are happy. And you know what happens when people are happy? They look forward to Monday—and, oh yeah, did I mention that the company is also probably profitably growing?

So, let me ask you this question: if you are a customer service agent at Spirit Airlines and there are policies you must follow with no exception, how do you feel about that? Well, you probably feel like, "They don't trust me enough to make a decision that is in the best interest of the company." Now, think about how differently you'd feel if your employer told you, "Here is a guideline, but we believe in you, we think you're a smart individual who can make smart decisions that are in the best interest of the customer and the company, so you're empowered to decide." Which approach would make you feel better about your job? And which workplace would make you more likely to look forward to Monday?

Let's take it one step further. Let's say you work for Spirit Airlines, and this big, bad story breaks. On Friday night you go out to dinner with all of your friends, and the first thing they want to talk about is, "Hey, Sally, don't you work for Spirit Airlines? Can you believe your company wouldn't refund a $147 ticket for a dying Vietnam veteran?" What are you going to say? How is that going to make you feel about the company you work for? And how in the world is that going to make you look forward to Monday? It's not. That's why the language that we use is so important to creating an environment that really attracts great people.

Also, don't forget communication is a two-way street, and you must do more listening than talking.

I CALL IT THE GOLDEN RATIO: CEOS AND LEADERS SHOULD BE LISTENING 70 PERCENT OF THE TIME, AND ONLY TALKING 30 PERCENT OF THE TIME.

I call it the *golden ratio*: the CEOs and leaders should be listening 70 percent of the time, and only talking 30 percent of the time. You learn a lot more by listening than you do by talking. Being listened to *is* empowering. When your team members feel as though they've been heard, it makes them feel better. It makes them feel like they are valued. When people feel valued it leads to happiness. When people are happy, they look forward to coming in on Monday morning. When your team members are happy, they take good care of your customers. When your customers are well taken care of, they tell their friends, they pay their bills on time, and magic happens . . . your company experiences profitable growth! BAM!

Every leader on our team aims to have one in-depth conversation every week with one direct report. This is called a Start-Stop-Keep conversation, another gem from Verne Harnish's book *Scaling Up*. The conversation goes like this: "Bill, what should the company start doing, what should the company stop doing, and what should the company keep doing?" Now it might not be the company, it might be the department, but by having the Start-Stop-Keep conversation, what you're doing is listening. You're getting feedback. The more listening you do, the better the decisions you make will be received. And the key to succeeding on your march to your BHAG is the ability to make decisions for the company that people readily embrace rather than resist and fight.

At Advantage, we have three priorities of our Leadership Team. In most businesses, there are three key stakeholders: the shareholders/investors, the employees, and the customers.

In the Advantage ecosystem, as described earlier, there are two other stakeholders in the business that we consider. One is vendors/partners/suppliers. The other is the community (communities) in which the business is located. But let's just take those three main groups: shareholders, employees, and customers. Most companies put the interest of the shareholder first. And there are a lot of people who believe that the sole function of business is to make money, and to maximize profit at any and all reasonable costs. Many people call that *shareholder maximization*. So, the shareholder comes first, the customer comes second, and then usually at the bottom of that pyramid is the employee.

At Advantage, we flipped the pyramid. Our Leadership's Priorities are, number one, take care of the team member. And the number-one goal at Advantage for our leadership team is what we call "team member Happiness."

I realize that statement probably has some of you rolling your eyes, because for a lot of us, business is all about being tough and making hard decisions. Well, that's baloney. Our philosophy is that if you take

LEADERSHIP'S PRIORITIES

TEAM MEMBER HAPPINESS
Build an Advantage in which our people love what they do and look forward to Monday.

MEMBER SUCCESS
Provide world-class service to our Members. Make the success of their business our business. Create a swarm of Raving Fans that goes viral.

PROFITABLE GROWTH
Serve more Members, reach more people, and have a bigger impact.

Advantage Leadership Priorities.

care of your team members, then they're going to be happy. For Advantage, we're a service-based company, which means our Members interact daily with our team members. And if our team members are positive and upbeat, happy and exceptionally competent and skilled, then our Members are going to have a great experience and they're going to have a book they're proud of. If your customers are successful and happy, they're going to repurchase and/or recommend. And if your customers are repurchasing or recommending, your company is going to grow.

Team member happiness is where it starts; creating an environment in which our people look forward to Monday results in Member (Customer) Success, and that's how we create a swarm of raving fans (delighted Members). Creating a swarm of raving fans leads to repurchase and recommendation. Repurchase and recommendation leads to Profitable Growth. And why do we want to profitably grow? *Because we want to serve more Members and have a bigger impact on the world.* If you see the priorities of your leadership team through that lens, business is much more productive, much more fun, and yep . . . people look forward to Monday, too!

NET PROMOTER SCORE

If you want your people to look forward to coming to work on Monday, you greatly improve your chances when you make a commitment to be a business that provides world-class customer service. Why is having great customer service such a reliable predictor of team member happiness? When your customers hate you, it's tough to get excited about going to work, because you know your day is going to be spent fighting fires and trying to appease unhappy customers—and that's not much to look forward to.

On the other hand, when you are genuinely invested in great customer service—when the ethos of the company is "How do we surprise, delight, and exceed the expectations of our customers?"—going to work is a pleasure, because you know you'll have the opportunity to make someone's day. Even if you screw up—and you will —or when things go wrong—and they will—you're going to be empowered with the support and resources to make that bad situation better and take great care of your customers.

If you're going to become a customer service-forward business, which I believe is one of the best moves you can make toward creating a TGIM workplace, you've got to be able to measure how well you're doing. Two yardsticks we use at Advantage to measure our effectiveness are Raving Fans and the Net Promoter Score.

What are Raving Fans? Authors Ken Blanchard and Sheldon Bowles wrote a book called *Raving Fans* back in the 90s; they defined a raving fan as a customer or client that is so pleased and delighted with the work your company has done for them that they effectively become your greatest sales ambassadors, promoting your business to everyone they know. When you become a customer service-forward business, you create a swarm of these raving fans, and they will generate referrals and introductions for you like nobody's business.

One small way in which you can measure how you're doing at creating your own raving fan base is to look at the amount of fan mail your company receives. At Advantage, we get a ton of fan mail; from thank you notes, greeting cards, even invitations to birthday parties, weddings, and bar mitzvahs. And gifts flow in, too; flowers, Edible Arrangements, and care packages of the things our clients' companies manufacture. In effect, these are "love letters," and we proudly display them all over our offices. When somebody pays your business for a product or service AND sends you love letters, that's a pretty good sign that you're serving that customer well. Your team members are going to be a lot more excited to come to work on Monday if your business gets fan mail, not hate mail. Where would you rather work?

The Net Promoter Score, or NPS, is a more scientific measure of how customer service-forward your business is. The Net Promoter Score is the most straightforward and simple way in which to measure customer satisfaction, because it relies on the answer to one simple question: On a scale of 1 to 10, how likely are you to introduce us to a friend or colleague? We ask that question to our Members every month. Every month we tabulate our Net Promoter Score, track it, and post it all over our offices so our team knows how we're doing.

The goal is to slowly but surely increase your Net Promoter Score. If your Net Promoter Score today was a 20, how can you grow your average score up to a 25 over the next six months? Once you're at 25, how do you increase that average score to a 30? Those companies whose customer service is recognized as the gold standard—Disney, Apple, Chick-fil-A, or Southwest Airlines for instance—will typically have Net Promoter Scores in the 60's. If yours is in the 40's or 50's, you're doing very well. If you want to be a company whose people look forward to Mondays, this is another powerful driver to get you to greatness.

Opposite: An graphic p throughou office and up after each su

SHOULD WE SURVEY OUR STAFF

Advantage | **Forbes**Books

RAVING**FANS**
REPORT

UPDATED:

RAVING FANS

PASSIVES

CURRENT NPS

DETRACTORS

WHAT IS
NPS?

50-80+: WORLD CLASS
20-49: GOOD
1-19: AVERAGE
-100-0: POOR

The **Net Promoter Score** is calculated by subtracting the percentage of detractors from the percentage of promoters, yielding a score between -100 to 100. A score of -100 means every respondent is a detractor while a score of 100 means everyone is a promoter. NPS is an indicator of your company's health and is the first step to improving your customer's loyalty.

THE FORMULA:
% PROMOTERS
- % DETRACTORS

NPS

DETRACTORS							PASSIVES		PROMOTERS	
0	1	2	3	4	5	6	7	8	9	10

BENCHMARKING
How our score compares
to leading businesses.

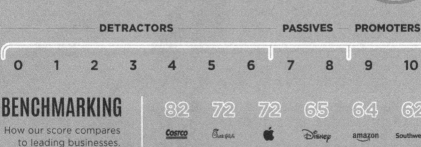

82	72	72	65	64	62
Costco	Chick-fil-A	🍎	Disney	amazon	Southwest

CHAPTER 8

RECRUI
THE BE

"IF EACH OF US HIRES PEOPLE WHO ARE SMALLER THAN WE ARE, WE SHALL BECOME A COMPANY OF DWARFS. BUT IF EACH OF US HIRES PEOPLE WHO ARE BIGGER THAN WE ARE, WE SHALL BECOME A COMPANY OF GIANTS."

—DAVID OGILVY

RECRUITING THE BEST

IF YOU WANT YOUR PEOPLE TO

look forward to Monday, one of the greatest factors in team member happiness is having A-player co-workers. If your colleagues are idiots or slackers who can't or won't competently do their jobs, what happens? The work that a co-worker was supposed to do ends up on your desk! When a professional doesn't have confidence in his or her colleagues, it makes work miserable. It makes work stressful. It makes work overwhelming. Most CEOs don't stop to calculate the true cost of having B- and C-players on their team, but the quality of the people you bring into your company has a direct result on the happiness and satisfaction of the team members.

The hiring success rate in businesses is abysmal. Forty-eight percent is the average success rate of hiring, which means one out of every two people you hire won't be there in a year. Unless you're looking for short-term team members, those aren't great odds for company success. If you calculate the cost of hiring the wrong person, you would be shocked to see how much money you're flushing down the toilet in the process.

If hiring is so important, then why aren't we better at it? There's a reason why the hiring success rate is only 48 percent. Most CEOs unknowingly follow the mantra, "Hire quickly, fire slowly." That's the opposite of what successful CEOs do, which is, "Hire slowly, fire quickly." Hiring the best takes longer, and you will save gobs of money in the long run if you insist on thoroughly searching, sifting, sorting, and vetting, and ultimately only hiring A-players.

MOST CEOS UNKNOWINGLY FOLLOW THE MANTRA, "HIRE QUICKLY, FIRE SLOWLY." THAT'S THE OPPOSITE OF WHAT SUCCESSFUL CEOS DO, WHICH IS, "HIRE SLOWLY, FIRE QUICKLY."

Why does hiring an A-player takes so much longer than hiring a B- or a C-player? Well, there are a lot more B- and C-players than there are A-players. Think about competitive athletics; on any sports team, there are usually one, two, maybe three all-stars and then there's everybody else. Sure, you've got to be pretty good to begin with to make it to the major leagues, but there are still only a few all-stars on that major-league team. The reason is because all-stars aren't born every day. They're special people and they're rare. B- and C-players are much more plentiful.

A-players perform at a high level when they're happy, which usually means the company they're performing for is also happy, and when the company is happy and the team member is happy, it's highly unlikely that the A-player will be looking for a new career. The B-players or the C-players may be okay performers, or maybe not so great. They're probably going to be unhappy, and the people employing them are going to be unhappy, so those B- and C-players spend a good bit of their time on job boards looking for the next best thing. The other thing to remember about B- and C-players is they rarely see their own poor performance as their responsibility, so they are more apt to have a philosophy that the grass is always greener on the other side. If you look at someone's resume and see that they've jumped around a lot, meaning they were at Company A for two years, they were at Company B for one year, they were at Company C for three years, they were at Company D for fourteen months, then they were at Company E for eighteen months, that's probably an indication this is a B-player at best, but more likely a C-player.

GIVEN THAT THE PEOPLE YOU ATTRACT AND RETAIN WILL HAVE MORE IMPACT ON THE SUCCESS OF YOUR BUSINESS THAN ANYTHING ELSE, RECRUITING TRULY IS THE NUMBER-ONE JOB OF THE CEO AND THE SENIOR LEADERSHIP TEAM.

• •

Given that the people you attract and retain will have more impact on the success of your business than anything else, recruiting truly is the number-one job of the CEO and senior leadership team. Unfortunately, most businesses big enough to have an HR department (or as I call it, "team member success") or an HR manager will delegate the responsibility of recruiting to HR. That's okay if it's an entry-level or associate position, but for strategic or executive positions in a company, it is the job of the CEO or another senior leader to lead that recruiting and hiring effort. Why is recruiting the number-one job of the CEO, specifically for key positions of importance? Simply because nobody can sell the company better than the CEO. *Nobody.* That's why he or she should be reaching out, recruiting, and finding the best talent. The CEO will

ALWAYS get better people to respond than a recruiter or HR manager will.

At Advantage, we have an expectation that every new hire must make the company better. Let's say that, on a scale of 1 to 10, the collective quality of the people in our organization is a 9.1. When we hire, we only want to hire people that are a 9.2 or better because when we add a new person to our team we want that person to raise the overall quality. That's an expectation every CEO should have.

LET'S SAY THAT, ON A SCALE OF 1 TO 10, THE COLLECTIVE QUALITY OF THE PEOPLE IN OUR ORGANIZATION IS A 9.1. WHEN WE HIRE, WE ONLY WANT TO HIRE PEOPLE THAT ARE A 9.2 OR BETTER BECAUSE WHEN WE ADD A NEW PERSON TO OUR TEAM WE WANT THAT PERSON TO RAISE THE OVERALL QUALITY.

Say you're trying to find a sales all-star for your sales team and there's an A-plus salesperson working for your competitor. This individual brings in multiple millions of dollars in business every year; she's respected by her peers, she's respected by her competitors, and she's a gem. Let me ask you—what's going to make a bigger impression on this woman? A call from the HR manager—or a call from the CEO personally reaching out to say, "Hey, Sally. This is Bill Smith over at XYZ Company; I've always admired your great work. I'm sure you're not interested in leaving your company, but if by chance you'd ever be open to a conversation I'd love to take you out for a cup of coffee to tell you about some of the neat things we're doing at my company and share with you how perhaps you could be a part of it."

Every CEO has what President Teddy Roosevelt famously called a *bully pulpit,* or a position of influence. The smart CEO knows how to effectively leverage his or her bully pulpit. Every CEO has a limited amount of time in which they can use that bully pulpit, and the wisest ones use it in the most impactful areas. Recruiting and hiring A-players is one of the most impactful areas. That's why every CEO, and really every member of a senior leadership team, should be spending at least 10 percent of their time on recruiting.

My friend Jack Daly likes to ask his clients the question, "Who's in your pipeline?" When he asks that question, he's not referring to what prospects are in your sales pipeline. He's asking, "Who is in your talent pipeline?" If one person on your team left tomorrow, you should have two, three, or four names already on your short list you could call and say, "We'd like to talk to you about this new opportunity." Most businesses don't have a pipeline of talent, period.

Here's why this is such a problem: say I'm the manager and Bill walks into my office and presents his letter of resignation, catching me completely off guard. He gives me two weeks notice. That night, after everybody's left the office, I feverishly begin building a job description from scratch, because I didn't prepare any job descriptions ahead of need. The next morning I'm going to ask my secretary to go post it on LinkedIn and Indeed, and see what we get. Remember, too, that it's generally the B- and C-list players who are trolling the job boards, not the A-players. After a few days, I have thirty to forty resumes and I'm feeling pretty good. I've got about an hour to go through these, so I'm spending about two minutes on each resume. I have two piles, a "keep" pile and a "trash" pile. I've got seven keepers. I hand them to my secretary, and ask her to call them and set up in-person interviews. I decide to stack them all up in one afternoon, and spend thirty minutes with each of them. After that first round of interviews, I narrow it down to the best two, and ask a colleague to interview my two top choices. I am in a major rush to fill Bill's job before he goes, because I know if he leaves before I find someone, his work

Topgrading Hiring Process

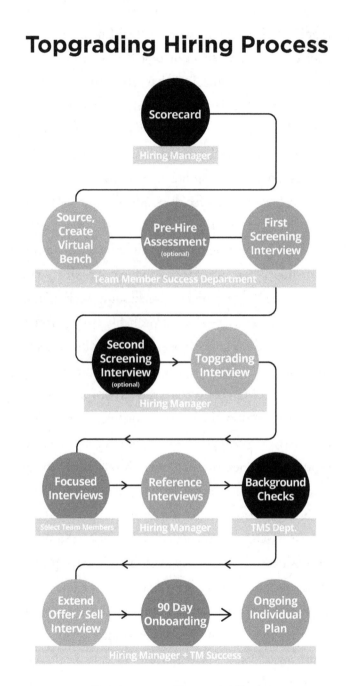

This is the process we utilize to recruit A-Players.

is going to become my work. When I make my final choice, I will have spent at best five to ten minutes reviewing their resume, I will have spent thirty minutes interviewing them in person, I will have had one other person interview them, and now I'm going to welcome them to the team. It's practices like this that make the success rate of hiring in business so low.

So how do you fix this? You fix this by being proactive, by recruiting 24/7. I said earlier that I want every CEO, every member of a senior leadership team, to spend 10 percent of their time recruiting. It's not going to be 10 percent every week; some weeks it'll be 20 percent, other weeks it'll probably be 5 percent. Maybe some weeks it's 0 percent. The point is, every single month an executive is spending time thinking about and having conversations with people they can potentially add to their talent pipeline, even if they don't have an open position. There is a crazy misconception in business that you can only talk to somebody about a job if there is presently a job opening. That's head-trash you must completely eliminate. The best, most successful entrepreneurs and CEOs are recruiting for positions that don't yet exist. They're having conversations with people who may not ever join their company. But you don't know unless you have the conversation. For the people who might join their company, it could be six months out, a year out, two years out. If they're truly an A-player and happy where they are, it's unlikely they're going to just jump ship immediately when you call them. It takes time. You've got to sell them, and this is not a quick sale. This is a long, drawn-out sale.

THE BEST, MOST SUCCESSFUL ENTREPRENEURS AND CEOS ARE RECRUITING FOR POSITIONS THAT DON'T YET EXIST.

But if you hire the right person, it could have a multi-million-dollar impact on your business, and that's where entrepreneurs and CEOs make the big mistake. They will spend hours upon hours working on a deal or a sale that they're trying to make. Yet they won't spend more than half an hour or so interviewing a person who's coming into their business. I would argue that the monetary impact on their business could be much higher with the person they're about to hire than the sale or deal they're trying to make. But most people are shortsighted and dramatically underestimate the cost of hiring the wrong person and the positive impact of hiring the right person.

I'm a huge college football fan. My team, the Clemson Tigers, is no different than any other major college football program in America, because the head coach is recruiting 365 days a year. Even during the season, he is recruiting. The head coach is the one who's getting on airplanes. He's the one who's getting in his car and leading home visits with families for the top recruits. Think about this for a minute: Dabo Swinney, the head coach of the Clemson Tigers football team, is recruiting today for the class he's going to sign two years from now! So, Dabo is building a pipeline of talented players who aren't even going to enroll at Clemson for another two years. How crazy is that? And Dabo's the one who's talking to players and their parents. Dabo's the one who's getting on an airplane and going to visit with them in person. His assistant coaches are recruiting, too, but if it's a five-star recruit, you'd better darn well believe that the CEO of the Clemson Tigers football team, the head coach, is going to be heavily involved. Dabo's ability to recruit better than his competition led him and the Tigers to a 2016 and 2018 National Championship.

When I ask you who's in your pipeline, you should be able to answer and give me a long list of people. The job of the CEO is to plan for the unexpected. If you lose people unexpectedly and you don't have a deep bench, you're in a tough position. You want to have your pipeline of talent, hoping that you never need to reference that pipeline unless you're adding new positions. But you must be prepared, nonetheless.

I told you that the hiring success rate in business is 48 percent, which means that one year from the date in which you hire someone, there's effectively a 52 percent likelihood that person is not going to be in your company. At Advantage, our goal is a 90 percent chance that person is with our business one year after we hire them. There's always going to be some chance they're not, and that's what that 10 percent accounts for. But if we're 90 percent certain, then we feel really good. That has been the foundation of our hiring philosophy.

Geoffrey Smart's book *Who* outlines the method for attracting and recruiting A-players. It's the method we've integrated at Advantage, and it's a method that works. The basis of it is this: *always have a pipeline and always be recruiting 365 days a year.* At Advantage, that philosophy runs through the entire organization. If you visit the careers page on our website, you'll notice there are dozens of positions currently open. We're not immediately prepared and ready to hire thirty people tomorrow, but we know that for many key positions you always want to have the door open. These are crucial areas of operation in which we need a lot of talented people, such as sales professionals, editors, and graphic designers. There are other positions that we intend to hire six months from now, and we know that if we want to get the right person we need to begin the process today. We're very strategic and we're very proactive with recruiting and hiring, beginning the recruiting and hiring process well before we actually want that person to walk into our door for the first time as an Advantage team member.

I want every entrepreneur and CEO to hire proactively, rather than reactively. Ninety percent of hires in America are reactive, not proactive decisions. When you do something reactively, you're doing it in a short, compressed period of time. You're doing it under duress, and it often leads to hiring mediocre people, at best. If I say to you, "Tell me who's in your talent pipeline," based upon your answer, I can predict where your company will be two years from today.

LinkedIn has a useful recruiter platform that can be a gold mine for hiring. There's a Recruiter Lite addition that's part of the premium service and there's a full-blown Recruiter platform that's much more expensive. If your company is doing a lot of hiring, buying the full-blown LinkedIn Recruiter platform makes sense.

To find the best people, you often have to poach them from another business. While that may sound sneaky or mean-spirited, the truth is, in business, as in sports, if you want to land the best player, chances are they're already signed with an existing team. You need to convince that player that if they come and play for your team they're going to be happier, perhaps earn more, and likely have a better chance at winning a national championship. A-players are rarely unemployed, so you have to reach out proactively, share your vision of where your business is going, and be able to convince them that working with you would be a wonderful decision for their professional life or would be a wise decision professionally.

A-PLAYERS ARE RARELY UNEMPLOYED, SO YOU HAVE TO REACH OUT TO THEM PROACTIVELY, SHARE YOUR VISION OF WHERE YOUR BUSINESS IS GOING, AND BE ABLE TO CONVINCE THEM THAT WORKING WITH YOU WOULD BE A WONDERFUL DECISION FOR THEIR PROFESSIONAL LIFE OR WOULD BE A WISE DECISION PROFESSIONALLY.

The big idea is that you hire slowly, and that means having in-depth, probing conversations with the people you're considering. You need to thoroughly examine their full professional background. You need to ask lots of questions. You need to be curious. When a candidate comes in to interview with us, they're going to spend anywhere from four to eight hours being interviewed. Those interviews are going to be with up to six different people. A lot of people say, "I don't have time for that." Wrong. What you don't have time for is the cost of waste, missed opportunities, and headaches that come with hiring the wrong person.

Pay attention to what people say when you ask them why they left their last job; Geoffrey Smart says you want to listen for whether people were *pulled up or pushed out.* If you hear people say, "My manager and I didn't see eye to eye on things," or, "I was looking for a new start," or, "The company merged with a competitor and my position was eliminated," those are all examples of people being pushed out. That's a bad sign if the majority of that candidate's job changes have come from being pushed out.

THE GREATEST PREDICTOR OF FUTURE SUCCESS IS PAST PERFORMANCE.

What you want to listen for is people being pulled up: "I got a promotion"; "My biggest competitor approached me and gave me the opportunity of a lifetime"; "My boss left to start his own company and asked me to join him"; "Our company opened up a new office and they asked me to lead the effort." The greatest predictor of future success is past performance. If in their previous position, they were kicking butt and taking names, then there's a good chance when they come to your business, they're going to do the exact same thing. If, on the other hand, they did a mediocre job wherever they were before, the chances are when they come to your business they're going to do the exact same kind of job for you.

If you have great team members, it's likely they're friends with other really great people. A-players tend to hang out with A-players. CEOs tend to be friends with other CEOs. Ditch-diggers tend to be friends with other ditch-diggers. It's not a question of right or wrong, it's just how it is.

If you're looking for an A-plus salesperson, the truth is that your current A-plus salesperson probably has a friend or friends that fit the bill. If you're looking to hire a Director of Finance and your CFO is an all-star, then she probably knows some people who would be well qualified for the position. Smart companies enlist their people to help them fill new positions. If your people look forward to Monday, they're going to want to invite their friends, acquaintances, and contacts to come join in on the fun. If, on the other hand, the culture of your company stinks, if people look forward to Friday and dread Monday, then they wouldn't wish that on their friends.

The number of internal referrals you're getting is a small indication of how you might be doing on the culture side. At Advantage, we have a $5,000 referral bonus, which means if you refer a candidate that we end up hiring, we pay the referring team member $5,000. The $5,000 is broken into three payments; five hundred dollars paid after the first ninety days, $2,000 paid after the first year, and $2,500 paid after Year 2. The reason we spread it out is to ensure this person is a committed player who can contribute long term. If you're hiring great people, then the probability of them being there in two years is high. For a team member who's making $50,000 per year, that bonus is 10 percent of their annual pay. That's real money, and it's something I would encourage other businesses to do. Now that we've discussed the importance of finding the best, let's turn the page and talk about what it takes to keep the best.

Advantage A-Player
Referral Bonus
Program.

Advantage. | **Forbes**
THE BUSINESS GROWTH COMPANY | Books

"A-Player" Referral Bonus
How to Earn $5,000 For Referring an A-Player

Who? This is the most important question we will ask and answer on our Road to 1,000. Over the next 5 years, we expect to add 50+ new team members. With every new person that joins our team, the quality and caliber should rise.

Finding great team members is just as difficult as finding great authors. Our best new authors are typically referrals from highly satisfied Advantage clients. The best new hires will likely come from highly satisfied team members.

We need YOU to help us find and hire THE BEST!

Recruiting "A-Players" is a full-time job, and a job that we need every team member of the Advantage team engaged in. We need your help identifying and finding the best new additions to our team.

WHAT IS AN A-PLAYER?

A candidate who has at least a 90% chance of achieving a set of outcomes that only the top 10% of possible candidates could achieve.

HOW DOES THE A-PLAYER REFERRAL BONUS WORK?

1 Refer or introduce a candidate to Advantage for an open or non-open position

2 Articulate to the Hiring Manager why this person is an "A-Player" and why they would be an invaluable addition to our team

3 If your referred candidate is hired, you receive a bonus, paid in 3 installments:

$ When the candidate celebrates their 90-day anniversary, $500 is paid

$$ When the candidate celebrates their 1-year anniversary, $2,000 is paid

$$$ When the candidate celebrates their 2-year anniversary, $2,500 is paid

CHAPTER 9

RETAIN THE BE

"THE EMPLOYER GENERALLY GETS
THE EMPLOYEES HE DESERVES."

—J. PAUL GETTY

RETAINING THE BEST

IN THE LAST CHAPTER, WE TALKED

about the importance of recruiting the best—but all of the effort you put into recruiting dies in vain if you're not able to keep great people. Having a revolving door of A-players does you no good. Why is it so important to keep the best people? Businesses flourish and thrive when there is continuity in key positions. The amount of knowledge and intellectual capital that somebody develops working in a business cannot be underestimated. When an A-player walks out of the door, whether it be three years, five years, or ten years from now, all those years of experience, intellectual capital, and institutional knowledge walk out the door too. That's a tremendous loss.

Most fast-growing businesses encounter resistance from current team members that goes like this: "The company is so focused on hiring new people that sometimes they forget about the people they already have." It's easy to understand their concern; it's a lot like the anxiety a former only child feels when Mom and Dad bring home the new baby. It's natural for your first child to feel a little let down and left behind when the new baby is getting all the attention.

The same thing happens in business. When you're growing really fast and the CEO and senior leadership team are heavily focused on recruiting and onboarding, it's only natural that your current team members may feel they've been forgotten about, and that the new people get all of the attention. For some people, there's a feeling of resentment: "Wait a minute. I've been with you for the last five years. I'm the one who helped us get to where we are today. What are we, chopped liver? You spend more time with the new people that haven't done squat than you do with us!" For any business that's growing the right way, the reality is the business values more tenured team members just as much as new team members. The key is ensuring that long-tenured team members feel valued. In this chapter, I provide a few different examples of how we work to retain our A-Players.

SCORECARDS

The number one tactic to retain an A-player is to have and communicate clear expectations. That seems simple on the surface, but the truth is most businesses don't do a very good job of this. If you walk into a business and ask people, "What's expected of you? What are your accountabilities? How is your performance

Team Member Scorecard						
Team Member:	John Doe	**Department:**	Publishing	**Year:**	2018	
Title:	Project Manager	**Manager:**	Adam Witty	**Hire Date:**	1-12-2016	
	Area		Annual	Pts Avail	Actual	Pts Awarded
A Player Outcomes	Professional Development Hours		120	10		
	Department Books Published		184	20		
	Projects under Budget		100%	15		
	% of priorities completed for you and your direct reports		75%	10		
	Reprint Budget [1]		<$5K	10		
	Member Calls		200	10		
Advantage Values	Create an environment that breeds greatness			5		
	Make a Difference			5		
	Build the Advantage Family			5		
	Take Initiative and Be Resourceful			5		
	Commit to Lifelong Learning			5		
Competencies	Exemplary attention to detail					
	Organization and planning					
	Proactivity—act without being told what to do					
	Positive communication and attitude					
	Leadership					
	TOTAL			100	0	0

Sample excerpt of a team member scorecard.

evaluated?" 60–70 percent of people will shrug their shoulders and say, "Beats me. It's opaque. I'm a sales guy, so my job is to get sales." What's your number? "I don't know. As much as I can." Well, "as much as I can" isn't a number. Or if you're a graphic designer and I ask you how many book covers you're supposed to design in a year—"I don't know." What happens if you don't hit that number? "I don't know." What happens if you exceed that number? "I don't know." That opacity is detrimental to a business.

One of the suggestions that Geoffrey Smart makes in his book *Who* is to create a scorecard before you hire someone. That scorecard, which also serves as a job announcement, clearly articulates to the person you're aiming to hire exactly what his or her responsibilities are if they join your company. More than simply explaining what those responsibilities are, it explains exactly what the three, four, or five outcomes are that the person must accomplish. Here's the magic of it; before they even apply for a job at your company, they're going to know what their expected outcomes are, so if they don't think they can do the job, they're not even going to apply.

Why is that so cool? Because it's going to save you a tremendous amount of time and energy in talking to people you don't need to consider. B- and C-players will see the expected outcomes of the position and won't even apply. This is a VERY good thing.

What's the rub on the scorecard? The Negative Nancys will say, "Oh, it's so transactional." A family is a place where you are loved unconditionally regardless of your talent or ability—but a business doesn't work

A FAMILY IS A PLACE WHERE YOU ARE LOVED UNCONDITIONALLY REGARDLESS OF YOUR TALENT OR ABILITY—BUT A BUSINESS DOESN'T WORK THAT WAY. A BUSINESS IS A PLACE WHERE YOU ARE LOVED BASED ON YOUR ABILITY TO PERFORM AND MAKE THE DESIRED IMPACT IN THE BUSINESS.

that way. A business is a place where you are loved based on your ability to perform and make the desired impact in the business. If you're unable to do that, then you're given an opportunity to either correct it or choose another place to work. Businesses are meant to grow. Businesses are meant to be profitable. In order to grow and be profitable, businesses have to be well run. Being well run means having people who are accountable, able to accomplish their outcomes and the goals that are set in front of them. That's where the scorecard allows you to measure very specifically if people are achieving their outcomes.

WHEN PEOPLE CLEARLY KNOW WHAT IS EXPECTED OF THEM, THEY CAN COMPETENTLY PERFORM. WHEN PEOPLE DON'T KNOW WHAT IS EXPECTED OF THEM, THERE'S ALWAYS HEAD SCRATCHING AND FRUSTRATION, WHICH CAN LEAD TO LACKLUSTER RESULTS.

Here's the bottom line: if your team member does not know what his or her measurable goals are, then they're not going to know whether or not they're achieving these goals. You may think your team members would prefer the subjective touchy-feely, "Oh, we just want you to do your best," versus a scorecard that says, "You've got to do this, this, this, and this." But the fact is, when people clearly know what is expected of them, they can competently perform. When people don't know what is expected of them, there's always head scratching and frustration, which can lead to lackluster results.

PERFORMANCE REVIEWS

Reviews should be regularly scheduled. We do our reviews every six months. Some companies may choose to do them quarterly, but in order to have a well-executed review, you, the manager, must be prepared, and the team member that's being reviewed is also prepared. That takes time, and we found at Advantage, when we were doing quarterly reviews, the team wasn't as well-prepared as they should have been.

Here's my rule about reviews: there should be no surprises. Surprises and big problems come when you don't deal with problems when they're small. Problems come up every day, and most problems are small the first time they occur. When those small problems aren't properly dealt with, they grow. Eventually, that problem explodes. If there is a big surprise in a review, that means you, the manager, had an opportunity to share something with a team member early on and you chose not to. It's human nature to put off unpleasantness, but you're just letting something fester that will become more serious down the road.

The other important thing is giving every team member a line of sight, a clear view of how their performance impacts the business, and how they impact the company's ability to achieve its Big Hairy Audacious Goal. (We are going to speak in-depth about how to do this in the next chapter.) When somebody can't see their impact toward the BHAG, it can be depressing, dispiriting, and demotivating. But when your people have a line of sight, when they can see directly how what they do day in and day out affects the overall success of the company, you're going to get better performances and have happier and more fulfilled people.

CAREER PATHS PLANS

As a leader, part of your job is to be a steward for the people working in your organization. One of the responsibilities of that stewardship is to inspire your people to learn, grow, and develop in the time that they're with you. We believe that people engaged in learning, growth, and development are happier than

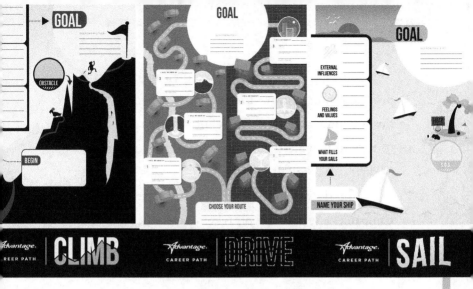

Career pathing visuals used in our office.

those who are stagnant. That's why we at Advantage craft a Career Path Plan for every team member to nurture that ongoing vibrant professional growth.

Granted, in an ideal world, if we have an A-player on our team, this'll be the last company they ever work for. But I'm realistic; I know that in today's world, even if someone is performing well and they're happy there's a high probability that at some point they're going to close the chapter of Advantage and open up a new chapter in their professional career.

At Advantage, creating the individual's Career Path Plan involves every manager having an in-depth, probing conversation with each person on their team to learn what their professional dreams and ambitions are, then work with them to craft a plan detailing what they should accomplish or learn over the next 24 to 36 months to help them get there. What skills do they need to attain? What experience do they need to get to the next level? Whether their objective is a promotion, or a move to a different department or business unit, we help them define the steps they need to take to prepare them for whatever the next phase of their career might be.

Why do we do this? One of the biggest reasons companies lose good people is because those employees feel like they have plateaued in their career. It's frustrating to people when they feel like they're treading water and going nowhere. That's particularly true of A-players who are driven and ambitious and likely to look elsewhere if they feel stymied. Your job as a leader is to do your best not to let that happen. Helping our people to create a Career Path Plan is one way we've found to keep them excited about coming to work on Monday.

RECOGNITION

If I were to walk into a business and say, "Raise your hand if you are receiving too much recognition from your company," how many people do you think would raise their hands? Can somebody be over-recognized? I suppose. I've never seen it. The goal is, if you're celebrating people's achievements, if you're consistently giving them the "Atta boy," that feeling of appreciation has a significant effect on retention.

People want to be recognized in different ways. Some people want to have their name called out in front of their peers. Others are mortified by that thought. The job of a great manager is to understand the recognition preferences of each individual.

Say you have an eager salesperson who had a bang-up, super quarter. The salesperson's numbers were off the charts. Many salespeople have egos; they like recognition, and they like to brag in front of their peers so people know they're the best. If, in a company meeting, the CEO calls out the person's name in front of everyone and asks that person to come to the stage or to the front of the room to award them a plaque, a trophy, or even just a picture of the CEO and the salesperson, it's going to go a very long way to making them feel valued.

On the other hand, let's say you have a graphic designer and she is an introvert. She hates all things related to public recognition for contributions. She has a family. She has two young daughters, and you know the one thing she'd like more than anything else is to have more free time to spend with her two little girls. If you called her to the front of the room for recognition in a company meeting, she'd be mortified. Alternately, you could call that graphic designer into your office and say, "Sarah, I can't tell you how much I appreciate all of your work this past quarter. The book covers you've designed have far exceeded our Members' expectations. I want you to know how much I appreciate your great work. As a small token of the company's appreciation, I want you to take next Friday off. I've got three tickets for you to take your daughters to the aquarium and I've arranged for you to have lunch on us." That's recognition that's meaningful and valuable for Sarah.

One of the things we do at Advantage is budget money every year for recognition, rewards, and incentives. Every department leader has a budget, and the expectation is that they use that budget. That budget could be used for Sarah's day at the aquarium with her kids. That money could be spent in recognizing your top salesperson (who you know is a golf nut) by sending him out for a day on the course.

We have a program called "Caught in the Act of Greatness," an idea inspired by ForbesBooks Member Jack Daly. When it comes to recognition, most leaders don't see everything that goes on in all parts of the business on a daily basis. It's impossible for someone to have that much visibility. "Caught in the Act of Greatness" is peer-to-peer recognition; when a colleague sees a coworker doing something great, they fill out a "Caught in the Act of Greatness" card. Then, every Tuesday during our weekly, company-wide all-hands huddle, the person publicly presents the recognition to this person who was caught in the act of greatness. Every quarter, everybody that has a card gets to put their card in a big lottery bin and we give away a grand prize. We've given away a 40-inch flat screen TV, an iPad, American

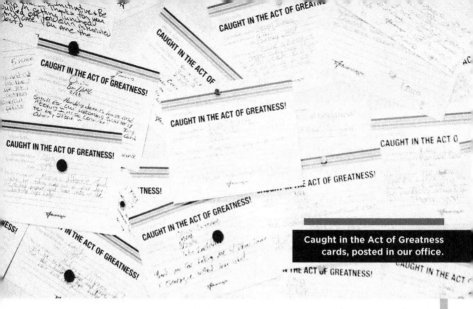

Caught in the Act of Greatness cards, posted in our office.

Express gift cards—all kinds of things. But "Caught in the Act of Greatness" is not about the prize. "Caught in the Act of Greatness" is about encouraging peers to recognize one another. That's so important because the CEO and the senior leadership team miss a lot of great things that deserve to be recognized.

PROFESSIONAL DEVELOPMENT

Another way to retain great people is to keep them learning and growing. At Advantage, one of our five core values is *commit to lifelong learning*. The truth is we only want to hire people who have a personal interest in ongoing professional development. To support that commitment, every team member is required to invest 120 hours annually on professional development. Much of that is supplied by Advantage. Each team member is granted $1,000 per year as a tuition credit they can use for any type of professional development. It could be attending a conference, buying books, a subscription to a publication or a magazine, or buying an online course, DVD or audio CD. It doesn't matter as long as what they're learning will have a tangible positive impact on their work at Advantage.

If a team member (say Leslie, who is a Marketing Coordinator) walks into your office next week and asks for a raise, what do you say? What criteria do you use to make that decision? At Advantage, we have a simple philosophy that goes something like this: "Leslie, it sounds like you'd like the company to increase its investment in you (i.e., the raise). First, share with me how you have invested in yourself." Lots of people want a raise because another year has ticked by. Many view a raise as something that is earned by tenure rather than through performance and growth. When a company gives a team member a raise, they're increasing their investment in that person. Smart investors invest in smart investment vehicles. If Leslie produces a list of the ten books she has read on marketing, the two conferences she attended, and the three podcasts she listens to every week, then you can feel confident you are making a smart investment by providing a raise. If Leslie looks at you with a blank stare when you ask what she has done to grow herself over the past year—well, if she hasn't invested in herself, why should you invest in her?

As the company scales up, it becomes impossible for the CEO to stay on top of this. That's why the CEO must make it a priority to train the leadership team of the company, to recognize, acknowledge, share gratitude, and appreciate the work of their people.

HANDWRITTEN NOTES

I love writing handwritten notes to our team members. We have custom 4-inch x 6-inch watermarked note cards with the Advantage logo at the top, and I frequently write handwritten notes of gratitude and appreciation or congratulations on a milestone or a job well done for people internally. People like them; in fact, many people like to hang and display those notes of appreciation. If that doesn't say something about the impact of a handwritten note, I don't know what does.

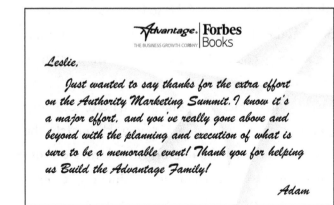

Leslie,

Just wanted to say thanks for the extra effort on the Authority Marketing Summit. I know it's a major effort, and you've really gone above and beyond with the planning and execution of what is sure to be a memorable event! Thank you for helping us Build the Advantage Family!

Adam

DREAM ON

A final thing we do to retain the best that I'll mention—and this is unique—is a program called "Dream On." When I started Advantage, I had a dream to build a globally recognized company. I believe that dreams are what sustain us. Dreams are what give people the energy to get up every morning. Without dreams, we have no hope, and without hope we have no reason to live. Everybody's dreams are different: my dream may be to build a globally recognized company that's best in its class. Another person's dream might be to travel the world. Someone else's dream might be to see all of their children graduate from college. There's no right or wrong to the dreams people have—the point is, everybody has them.

The founder of a business typically has a dream they're pursuing with that business. As the business grows, they hire people, and essentially convince other people to work toward that same dream. The Big Hairy Audacious Goal is so important because it outlines the vision (read: dream) of what the business is going to accomplish. It outlines the vision of where the business will be at a certain time in the future. Ideally, the people who come on board to join your company share that vision with you. Ultimately, the best and most productive organizations are those where the dream of the founder ultimately becomes the dream of everybody else working in the company,

A photo from a Rocky Mountain backpacking trip awarded to a team member. The inset shows the dream as it appears on his board.

Backpack in the Rockies.

ULTIMATELY, THE BEST AND MOST PRODUCTIVE ORGANIZATIONS ARE THOSE WHERE THE DREAM OF THE FOUNDER ULTIMATELY BECOMES THE DREAM OF EVERYBODY ELSE WORKING IN THE COMPANY, TOO.

• •

too. Outside of that, every single person and every single business in the world has their own dreams, and it would be selfish of me as the CEO to think mine are the only dreams that matter.

Here's what we do to honor others' dreams: after a new team member has been with us for ninety days, we have our VP of team member success sit down with that team member and walk them through our Dreamboard Creation process, an exercise to help them identify their dreams. Then we design a 2-foot x 3-foot Dreamboard, a four-color graphic display of their dreams. We create two copies of this Dreamboard; one copy they can take home and one copy they can display at our office.

Dreamboards do two things: first, it allows every single team member every single day to acknowledge and look at their dreams, and it creates accountability to make sure that they're following those dreams. Second,

Actual Dream Boards of
Advantage team members.

it informs those around you about what you want to do. If nobody knows what your dreams are, nobody can help you. But if your friends and your colleagues know what your dreams are, then they can help, they can motivate, and they can be your cheerleaders.

I'll give you a great example. Let's say one of your dreams is to climb Mount Everest; that's a pretty big dream. If a colleague sees your Dreamboard, she might say, "You know, Tim, I've got a friend who lives out in California who climbed Mount Everest about three years ago. I'd be happy to introduce you guys. You might want to talk to him." Something as simple as that can make the difference between someone achieving their dreams, or not achieving their dreams. We create these Dreamboards because I want every person in the company to be aware of and looking at their personal dreams on a regular basis. Secondly, I want colleagues and members of our leadership team to know the dreams of our team members. If we know your dreams, then we can recognize and reward you in a way that will get you closer to achieving one of your dreams.

The final piece of the Dreamboard is something we call "Dream On." Dream On is a program where, randomly throughout the year, Advantage awards the dreams of A-players on our team. As an example, our President of Publishing had one of her dreams realized the day before Christmas a few years back. At the time she was awarded her dream, she'd been with Advantage for eight months, and she'd done an exceptional job. One of her dreams was to visit Ireland, so Advantage awarded her an all-expenses paid trip for two to Ireland to visit and stay in five different historic castles.

I had asked her to come into my office a few days before Christmas. I gave a little box to her and said, "Patti, thanks so much for all your hard work this year. This gift is a small token of my appreciation. Please don't open it until Christmas morning."

THE POINT ISN'T TO BUY PEOPLES' LOYALTY. IT'S TO RECOGNIZE AND REWARD, WHICH CREATES LOYALTY— THE BIGGER POINT IS HOW NEAT IT IS THAT THE COMPANY IS PROACTIVELY TAKING PART IN HELPING THEIR TEAM MEMBERS ACHIEVE THEIR DREAMS.

Christmas Eve, I get a phone call. My cell phone rings, but I'm on the phone, so I can't pick it up. Then, my desk phone rings, and I know it's her because we have caller I.D. Immediately, I knew she had opened the gift. So, I call her back. She's literally screaming: "I could barely sleep last night. I was wondering what was in that little box. I got up this morning and the kids were still in bed and I was in the kitchen, and I thought, it wouldn't hurt if I opened up this present on Christmas Eve. I woke up the neighbors. I woke up everybody in the house. I absolutely can't believe it. Thank you so much!"

Do you think she's committed? Yeah. She isn't looking to go anywhere else. The point isn't to buy peoples' loyalty. It's to recognize and reward, which creates loyalty—the bigger point is how neat it is that the company is proactively taking part in helping their team members achieve their dreams.

A photo from a Dream On trip to Ireland. The inset shows the dream as it appears on her board.

CHAPTER 10

MAKING
MEETIN
MEANIN

"AS CEO, REMEMBER,
MEETINGS ARE YOUR JOB."

—MARK RICHARDSON

MAKING MEETINGS MEANINGFUL

ASK ANYONE WHAT THE MOST-HATED

activity of their workweek is and chances are they'll say "meetings." Most of us see meetings as time drains, wasted effort in which nothing of value is accomplished. In most meetings, you walk into a room and sit down, people blather and blab, and at the end, whenever that end point is—though it usually goes over time—everybody gets up and walks out of the room as confused or more so than when they walked in. If your meetings follow this pattern, what's the likelihood that your people are going to say, "Thank Goodness it's Monday"? However, if you make meetings meaningful and productive, if you make them exciting, then you'll do a lot to increase and enhance the engagement of your team members.

The difference between a great meeting and a lousy one is largely preparation. Let's look at sports: you have a big game coming up, and the week before, you don't practice. You don't prepare, you don't study your opponent, and you walk onto the field and wing it. What are your chances of winning? Take a business example: you're a sales professional making a sales call. You don't know much about the prospect you're calling on; you have no clue why he's interested in talking to you in the first place. You walk into his office, you sit down, and you wing it.

THE DIFFERENCE BETWEEN A GREAT MEETING AND A LOUSY ONE IS LARGELY PREPARATION.

Sounds absurd, but honestly, that's what most leaders do when they run a meeting. They wing it, because preparation takes time. If you want to win the game on Saturday, then you have to prepare Sunday, Monday, Tuesday, Wednesday, Thursday, and Friday. If you want to have an effective sales call, then you must research your prospect and his or her needs, and figure out now what you have to offer that will make his or her life better.

Meetings are no different. If you want to have a really good meeting, you must prepare. You must have an agenda; you must share that agenda with attendees ahead of time. You must know the desired outcomes; what is it you want to accomplish? You must be

committed to making decisions at the end of the
meeting. You must be committed to recording the
decisions that were made and determining who is *ARE MEETIN*
responsible for doing what next. *A CHANCE TO INCREASE*
PERSONAL CONNECTION

Meetings should not be boring, and they won't
be if you include stories, anecdotes from customers
and team members, new information, and encourage
constructive conflict. If you have all of those elements,
and prepare well, then you can actually make meetings
meaningful and fun. Some of you may be surprised
at the inclusion of conflict in that list; conflict in a
meeting? It seems counterintuitive. The problem with
most meetings is that you walk into a room and for
sixty minutes everybody shakes their head in unison and
agrees with everyone, even though they secretly don't
agree. They don't want to speak their minds, because

MEETINGS SHOULD NOT BE BORING, AND THEY WON'T BE IF YOU INCLUDE STORIES, ANECDOTES FROM CUSTOMERS AND TEAM MEMBERS, IF YOU'VE GOT NEW INFORMATION TO SHARE, AND IF YOU ENCOURAGE CONSTRUCTIVE CONFLICT.

there isn't a high level of trust, and they don't want to create conflict. When people don't voice their opposition, but rather silently disagree with the decisions, they quietly sabotage the decisions after the meeting.

If you're talking about significant issues, you want to make sure everybody is contributing by providing feedback. You want to make sure that if people have concerns about the decisions that are being made or the direction in which something is going, they're confident and comfortable enough to speak up and share those concerns in a constructive fashion. If you have constructive conflict in your meetings, not only does more get done, but it's also energizing. Watching people disagree and debate in a constructive way is fun. If constructive conflict is a part of every meeting, not only do people actually want to go to the meetings to see what's going to happen, but it also allows people to get issues and concerns out on the table, and to come together on the decision that's been made before they walk out the door. This creates alignment within your organization and keeps communication open while allowing people to feel valued.

Too often, leaders use meetings to announce their plans: "Here's what we're doing. We're doing this, we're doing this, and we're doing this. You've got your marching orders. Goodbye." If these are valued team members and you're not asking them for feedback and insight, then effectively, you've hired them for their hands rather than for their head. If you're not tapping into their minds, their creativity and insights, you're missing out on all the good stuff that can thrust your business forward. Push for engagement: constantly solicit their feedback, and facilitate constructive conflict. Don't hesitate to bait people to disagree if you sense they don't fully buy into or support something.

OPEN AND HONEST COMMUNICATION IS PARAMOUNT. ONE THING EVERY CEO LEARNS THE HARD WAY IS THAT IT'S IMPOSSIBLE TO OVER-COMMUNICATE, ESPECIALLY IN FAST-GROWING BUSINESSES WHERE THERE'S LOTS OF CHANGE.

Open and honest communication is paramount. One thing every CEO learns the hard way is that it's impossible to over-communicate, especially in fast-growing businesses where there's lots of change. As the CEO, you will think the company is communicating at an adequate level, but when you ask your team, they will almost always say, "No, we are under-communicating."

Keeping that information flow open and moving is a never-ending challenge.

How can you open the lines of communication? Great meetings. Remember, as the leader, meetings are your job. The job of the CEO is to lead meetings that are engaging, interesting, and impactful. When people dread coming to your meeting, they tune out. They doodle and draw. Their mind is in another place. If the people you're asking to come to your meetings aren't there mentally, what's the point of holding the meeting?

Hosting good meetings requires preparation. It's the CEO's job to be prepared for the meetings. It's also the CEO's job to ensure members of the senior leadership team, who are also conducting meetings, are prepared and putting in the necessary time on the front end to ensure those meetings are successful. Having a regular schedule for meetings helps them stay focused and productive. There will always be ad hoc meetings called due to the kinds of unforeseen issues that arise in any organization, but certain meetings (leadership team meeting, the sales team meeting, the marketing team meeting, and the finance team meeting, etc.) should be held on regular schedules. Having good meeting rhythms is essential.

It's also vital to have someone in charge of each meeting, to make sure you stay on topic and adhere to a tight schedule. A good facilitator will cut people off if they go off on a tangent or exceed their time. If you don't have someone empowered to cut people off, your ninety-minute meeting becomes a two-and-a-half-hour meeting, which is why people resent meetings. This role is typically reserved for the facilitator. When conducting offsite strategic planning meetings, it's usually beneficial to have an outside facilitator so the CEO can more actively participate rather than play facilitator.

COMPANY BUSINESS PLAN REVIEW

At Advantage, we have a number of scheduled meetings to foster open and honest communication, each with specific goals and timelines. The first is called Business Plan Review (BPR), a weekly meeting of our senior leadership team. We meet for sixty minutes every Tuesday at 8:30 a.m. BPR is an idea I borrowed many years ago from Alan Mulally, the legendary CEO of Ford Motor Company who saved the company from bankruptcy and a government bailout. The concept of the meeting is simple: every week, each member of the senior leadership team has a slide. On that slide they have a red, yellow, or green indicator next to their key metrics for their department or business unit. Every week we can easily determine whether or not we're ahead of plan, behind plan, or right on plan. BPR has allowed us to get on top of small problems before they escalate. It has also created a wonderful vehicle

Breaking down the numbers at our Business Plan Review meeting. We do it every week.

for visibility, transparency, and accountability among all senior leaders.

DEPARTMENTAL BUSINESS PLAN REVIEW

Departmental Business Plan Review meetings—for our marketing team, our sales team, our publishing team, our finance team, and our operations team—are held weekly, typically for thirty to sixty minutes. The leader of each team, who also sits on our senior leadership team, conducts the meeting with the members of their department or business unit. The format is similar to a mini BPR.

Breakfast Like a Boss is our weekly All-Hands Huddle.

COMPANY ALL-HANDS HUDDLE

Every Tuesday at 9:30 a.m., the team gathers in our largest conference room for our All-Hands Huddle, which is a seven-minute information-sharing and recognition meeting. The purpose of this meeting is to provide visibility while creating alignment via a short overview of companywide progress toward key performance indicators (KPIs) and sharing of important wins and victories. We also announce birthdays, company anniversaries, and the weekly winner of the company Mustang (refer to chapter 5 for more on this.) This meeting serves as an early-week pit stop allowing us to check on numbers, celebrate victories and accomplishments from the past week, and look ahead to what's next.

I LIKE THIS

QUARTERLY PLANNING

In most organizations, execution planning is reserved for top managers and senior leaders within the company. Decisions are made, and then, like Moses coming down from the mountaintop with stone tablets, orders are delivered. To create better alignment among all team members within our company, we hold a half-day quarterly planning meeting every ninety days. This planning day runs from 8 a.m.–12 p.m. or 1–5 p.m. and is organized to be fun and motivational. The purpose of the meeting is to review results of our companywide performance from the previous quarter, share feedback on why we did or didn't achieve certain objectives, and gather everyone's wisdom in setting the companywide key priorities and targets for the upcoming quarter. This allows each team member to set their top three priorities that align with helping achieve company priorities.

QUARTERLY KICKOFF

We hold a two hour quarterly Kickoff (for the upcoming calendar quarter) and Business Plan Review for the immediately passed calendar quarter the first week of each quarter. The purpose of the meeting is to remind everyone how much we accomplished in the past quarter and celebrate victories while then turning our attention to the priorities of the new quarter.

If you've ever seen a town hall meeting, a politician is usually sitting on a stool in the front of the room and members of the audience ask questions. Once per quarter, I'm the lucky guy sitting on that stool!

As part of our Quarterly Kickoff, we also conduct a quarterly Business Plan Review where I share with all team members how the company is performing against our plan. We share this information to create a culture and environment of transparency. There's nobody in the corner office scheming to do things that'd hurt team members or the company. This is something we do to show our people we're all in this together, that the leadership team has everyone's best interests at heart, and the reasons behind our decision-making. When people are included, they're happier and they're more likely to look forward to Monday. When people feel like the company is hiding information, it breeds a culture of mistrust, which leads to lower levels of performance.

The Annual Kickoff is a way to celebrate the New Year, share information, and review goals for the four quarters ahead.

ANNUAL KICKOFF

Our Annual Kickoff falls in the second week of January, and it's a full day. It's a kickoff for the New Year and a way to share information, like company plans and priorities, with team members. Our annual kickoff also includes or Q1 Kickoff and Business Plan Review.

ADVANTAGESTOCK

AdvantageStock is our annual two-day companywide offsite, held in the second week of July each year. If our annual kick-off sets the tone, the direction, and the priorities for the year ahead, then AdvantageStock is a way for us to check in halfway through the year and communicate adjustments we're making. We invite speakers, hold training exercises, and play games that contribute to communication and team building. We also invite our Members to tell us, in their own words, how Advantage has positively impacted their lives and their businesses. It's easy for me to say we make a difference, but it's more meaningful when team members hear it from Members firsthand. This encourages people to get fired up about their work. AdvantageStock is also when we recognize team members for their incredible contributions. The first evening of AdvantageStock, we hold our annual awards banquet. During the ceremony, we acknowledge and recognize our team members for their contributions, and we have some special surprises too. AdvantageStock also includes our Q3 Kickoff and Q2 Business Plan Review.

In any business, I feel the more directly you can connect your customers or clients to your team members, the more you can paint the picture of what the company has meant to them. That's a really good thing.

Meaningful meetings that are fun, effective, and efficient have an impact on the goal of creating an environment where people say, "I'm looking forward to Monday."

Advantagestock 2017—note the palm trees! We celebrated that night with a luau.

CHAPTER 11

INVESTI
IN YOUR

G
PEOPLE

"WHEN YOU INVEST IN PEOPLE
AND LIFT THEM TOWARD
THEIR POTENTIAL, THEY
WILL LOVE YOU FOR IT."

—JIM ROHN

INVESTING IN YOUR PEOPLE

FOR MOST BUSINESSES,

whether you sell products or services, the largest line item on your profit & loss statement under the expense category is payroll. You have a choice as a CEO. You can consider that line item an expense, or you can consider that line item an investment you're making in your business to grow. You can view your team members as merely means to an end: "The fewer that I have, the better, and wouldn't business be great if I didn't have to have any at all?" On the other hand, you can have the attitude that being a manager and a leader is a noble profession, that it's an honor to have the privilege to give people the opportunity to make a living, to grow professionally, and to enhance their skills so when they leave your company they will be more polished, more knowledgeable, and more capable than the day they walked in your front door.

If you're a business owner and want to grow a business of any considerable size, then you're going to need a lot of people. If you don't like employees, it's going to be very difficult to build a world class organization of any significant size or scope. I'll also tell you that you might want someone else to be the CEO. It doesn't mean you can't be an entrepreneur, but it probably does mean you need to let someone else be the head of the company.

IF YOU WANT TO GROW YOUR BUSINESS, IT'S FAR MORE PRODUCTIVE TO HAVE THE ATTITUDE OF "MY PEOPLE ARE AN INVESTMENT" RATHER THAN "MY PEOPLE ARE AN EXPENSE."

. . . .

The most successful business owners are the ones who know their strengths and weaknesses. They know what activities give them joy and energy, and which activities drain them. If growing people is not something you derive satisfaction from, either find a new line of work, or find someone who does. I know many business owners who continue to wear the hat of CEO/ Head of Company, yet fundamentally dislike employees and everything that comes with them. If that's you, you are stunting the growth of your business. If you want to grow your business, it's far more productive to have the attitude of "My people are an investment" rather than "My people are an expense."

How do you invest in your people? I think the most meaningful investment any leader can make is providing education and professional development. At Advantage, we have five core values, one of which is *commit to lifelong learning.* That means if we invite you to join our team, we expect you to have a personal commitment to and interest in learning and growing. We shouldn't have to force it down your throat. We also expect the leaders of Advantage to invest in their people. My goal at Advantage is to have the most educated team in our industry.

As mentioned previously, we require every team member to complete 120 hours of professional development and continuing education per year. Additionally, every team member has a $1,000 per year credit that they can spend on classes, seminars, books, publications and online courses, as long as it's something that tangibly benefits the work they are doing at Advantage.

Some people use their continuing education credit for membership dues. For example, three people in our marketing team decided they wanted to join the American Marketing Association, so we paid the professional dues, and those three people are going to the American Marketing Association's annual conference. The first thought that some readers might

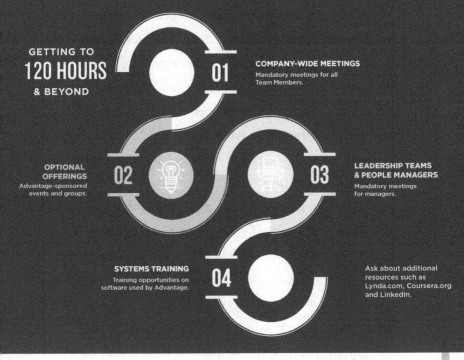

PROFESSIONAL
DEVELOPMENT

GETTING TO
120 HOURS
& BEYOND

01 COMPANY-WIDE MEETINGS
Mandatory meetings for all
Team Members.

OPTIONAL
OFFERINGS
Advantage-sponsored
events and groups.
02

03 LEADERSHIP TEAMS
& PEOPLE MANAGERS
Mandatory meetings
for managers.

SYSTEMS TRAINING
Training opportunities on
software used by Advantage.
04

Ask about additional
resources such as
Lynda.com, Coursera.org
and LinkedIn.

Internal graphic depicting professional development opportunities.

have is, "Adam, why in the world would I pay for my Marketing Director to be a member of AMA, which is filled with other companies that might want to poach and hire her away?"

Well, here's the deal. First, if people want to leave your company, then they're going to leave your company whether they're members of a professional organization or not. Second, the fact that your business is investing in their professional development and education goes a longer way than you may think. It creates loyalty and commitment. In addition, success leaves clues, and some of the best ideas that can innovate your business come from outside of your industry. In your industry, everybody has groupthink. If you encourage your team members to join professional organizations where they are meeting and networking and talking with people who do the same thing but in other industries, then the ideas they will learn and bring back can be profound.

Another way we invest in our people is with unique and interesting perks. If you want your workplace to be exciting and attractive, then you must show love in ways that let your people exercise initiative and make choices. You must do things that are unconventional. Now, granted, perks cost money; again, we have two ways to look at this. Do we want to look at it as an expense, or do we want to look at it as an investment? Remember, the cost of losing an A-player can be as much as one to four times that person's salary in time, lost productivity, lost opportunity, headaches and hassles. Are perks going to add to your expense tally? Yes. But if they allow you to retain great people, that expense becomes an investment that will pay off handsomely in retention and loyalty.

The investments you make in perks should be done intelligently. You can't do it all, so you have to be smart and pick and choose the perks that have the

PERKS & BENEFITS

SOME OF THE USUAL AND UNUSUAL WAYS WE SUPPORT OUR TEAM MEMBERS

EROUS VACATION	HEALTH BENEFITS	COMPANY-PAID LIFE INSURANCE	401K WITH COMPANY MATCH
N REIMBURSEMENT	WORK FROM HOME DAYS	HALF-DAY FRIDAYS IN AUGUST	WORLD CLASS OFFICE DOWNTOWN W/ PARKING
JAL DRESS CODE	$5,000 TEAM MEMBER REFERRAL BONUS	DREAMBOARD & DREAM ON	OPEN BOOK CO. W/ QUARTERLY TOWN HALL BY CEO
ABLE INVOLVEMENT	MAC COMPUTERS	NO QUESTIONS ASKED SPENDING (to surprise and delight our Members)	ANNUAL FLU SHOT

Team member perks as they appear on our website.

most impact. Here's a clue: it's more productive to ask your team members what they value most than it is to guess, because what they value most might surprise you.

WORK @ HOME DAYS

One popular perk we offer (depending on the role of the team member) are Work @ Home days. Every team member who is in good standing and is hitting his or her goals can work from home one day a week. Why is that so important to people? Because if the refrigerator repair man or the plumber is coming, if you're having new furniture delivered, if life needs to happen, then you can schedule those things on your Work @ Home day. We've found that most people are more productive at home than they are at the office, because there are no distractions. This also communicates a level of trust and empowerment.

HALF-DAY FRIDAYS

Another perk are Half-Day Fridays. During the month of August, when families are enjoying long weekends and vacations, we close at 12:30 p.m. on Fridays. For team members who want to take advantage of this flexible work schedule, we simply ask they work a 9-9-9-9-4 hourly schedule during the week. We are headquartered in Charleston, SC, which is a beach town. We have beautiful weather, the beach, boating, golf—it's also a time when a lot of people take family weekend trips. Half-Day Fridays makes that family time easier to find.

FIRST-CLASS FACILITIES

A first-class team deserves a first-class office, so we invest in having first-class facilities. I talk about sports a lot and I constantly hear college football and basketball coaches talk about the importance of having first-class facilities. Their rationale is that they're competing with other schools to land recruits. At my alma mater, Clemson University, they're competing with the University of Georgia, they're competing with Ohio State, they're competing with the University of Texas, they're competing with the University of Alabama and the list goes on. If a young recruit tours the football complex which was built in 1962 and hasn't been updated in forty years, that program will likely become much less attractive. When that same recruit goes to all of these other schools, they may see the Taj Mahal. As the head coach of your company, if you want to recruit and retain the best, your facilities must be competitive. If your office is a dump, it's harder to recruit great people. If your office is innovative, cool, well decorated, welcoming, and a fun, high-energy environment with lots of vibrant colors and nice furniture, then you've got a leg up over the guy whose office is in a dilapidated strip mall furnished with relics from 1982. If you want to create an environment that breeds greatness, place plays a big part.

IF YOU WANT TO RECRUIT AND RETAIN THE BEST, THEN YOUR FACILITIES MUST BE COMPETITIVE.

CHARITABLE INVOLVEMENT
AND COMMUNITY

We talked about Dreamboards and Dream On; we're also invested in charitable involvement as a way to team-build beyond the walls of our office and give back to the community. Charitable involvement is important, for a couple of reasons. Number one, I personally think it's the right thing to do. If a business exists in a community and is making a profit on the work being done there, then that business has responsibility to give back, to say thank you. You may agree or disagree, but another compelling reason to give back is that you'll find your team members care about it. When your team members go to a party with all their friends, invariably the topic of work comes up. Your team members are either proud of the company they work for and talk it up, or they're embarrassed by the company and do their best not to talk about it at all. As a CEO, are you doing things that make your people proud to work for your company? Charitable involvement is one of those things that makes your team members proud of the company they work for.

This doesn't have to require a huge investment of time or money. It could be volunteering a day with Habitat for Humanity and helping build a Habitat house. It could be making your business a drop-off location for the Toys for Tots toy drive and encouraging your team members to contribute. It could be asking everybody in the company to bring canned goods for Thanksgiving, having the company match what everybody brings, and then donating all of those canned goods to a local food bank. We do many of these things at Advantage, and our people are happy and proud to participate.

In addition, we do something special based upon the unique experience we have as a publishing company, called Advantage Impact. One thing every nonprofit needs help with is marketing and getting their story out to more people. On our website, we have a rolling call for entry, and every quarter we receive entries from people

who want to write and publish a book for their nonprofit. Everybody in the company gets to vote for their favorite entry, and once per quarter we publish a book at no charge for that nonprofit so they can use the book as a marketing tool to share their message with the world.

So, I ask you again: when your team members go to a party with their friends and the topic of work comes up, are they proud of the company they work for, or are they embarrassed? All of this plays a part in creating an environment where people look forward to Monday!

CHAPTER 12

LOVE

'EM

"A COMPANY IS STRONGER
IF IT IS BOUND BY LOVE
RATHER THAN BY FEAR."

—HERB KELLEHER

LOVE 'EM

I'M GOING TO END THE BOOK WITH

a pretty simple concept that in practice can be difficult for some. To create an environment that breeds greatness, to create an environment in which people say, "I'm looking forward to Monday"—at the heart of it all, there must be love. Herb Kelleher, the co-founder of Southwest Airlines, said, "A company is stronger if it's bound by love rather than fear." For those who are thinking, "Oh, here goes Adam, getting all touchy-feely," let's think about family for a minute.

If you are a member of a family that is bound by love, you care for each other, you want the best for each other, and you're honest and open with each other. You don't talk behind each other's backs, and you don't politicize or say negative things. If your family is a loving one, when you get invited to a family dinner, you look forward to going. If you grew up in a loving household, when you got out of school, you looked forward to going home.

If you were not as lucky and grew up in a family that was broken, negative, toxic and dysfunctional, my bet is when the school bell rang at 3 p.m., you would do anything possible to avoid going home. You'd play basketball, baseball, join marching band, go to a friend's house, or you might even stay in the library and study—anything to avoid having to go home.

A family bound by love is stronger than one not bound by love; families that are bound by love look forward to spending time with each other. If that's true for a family, why can't it be true for a business? If you create a company that is bound by love, you are well on your way to creating an environment people look forward to returning to. If, on the other hand, your company is toxic, laying people off left and right, firing people at random, having a hard time meeting performance goals, not growing but remaining stagnant—more likely than not, people will dread the idea of going to work when Monday morning rolls around.

If the CEO has truly created an environment of love and support for one another among his or her team, it can make all the difference in the world. If you want passionate and engaged people working with you, you really do have to love 'em. You must believe everybody on your team is unique and valuable. You must believe every person on your team deserves to be treated with dignity and respect.

I spoke earlier about people on a team who are producing results but not living the values of the company. A perfect example is the top-producing sales rep, the guy everybody on the sales team recognizes as the pacesetter, yet he's a complete jerk. Nobody likes

IF THE FOUNDER, THE CEO, THE HEAD OF THE COMPANY, HAS TRULY CREATED AN ENVIRONMENT OF LOVE AND SUPPORT FOR ONE ANOTHER AMONG HIS OR HER TEAM, IT CAN MAKE ALL THE DIFFERENCE IN THE WORLD. IF YOU WANT PASSIONATE AND ENGAGED PEOPLE WORKING WITH YOU, THEN YOU REALLY DO HAVE TO LOVE 'EM.

. . . .

him. He's disrespectful. He thinks he's better than everybody else. He's unwilling to help and share what he knows with his colleagues, and the boss tolerates him simply because he brings home the bacon. If it weren't for this guy's stellar sales numbers, he'd have been fired months ago. This is the great conundrum for any leader, because when you keep these people on board, you self-sabotage the success of the business long term, because you're suggesting that results are more important than attitude, and as long as you hit your numbers, you can get away with this kind of crap.

Yes, results are important, and if you do it right, you can have positive results *and* a great culture—it doesn't have to be one or the other. If you want to create an environment where people feel loved and appreciated and you don't fire this arrogant, egotistical sales guy, you're communicating subtly and subliminally that his behavior is acceptable. That is a very dangerous thing to do. The imperative of the leader is to make tough decisions that are in the best interests of the team. I want you as a leader to think a year, two years, five years down the road, not just one month or one quarter down the road. If you only look one month down the road, it makes absolutely no sense at all to let the egotistical jerk sales guy go, because he's your top producer. But if you think about the negative impact he has on you building a world-class sales culture, then he's a detriment.

People in the workforce today are looking for growth and development. They're also looking for coaching. Whenever I am personally involved in interviewing a candidate at Advantage, I like to say, "Listen, Sam. If everything works out, it certainly would be a pleasure to have you join our team. I can tell you this, if you're performing and we're happy with you, and on the other side, you're happy with us, my hope is that this will be your last job interview." I'll say, "I'm not hiring you with an expectation you'll commit to us for life, but if everything goes well and you're happy and we're happy, that's certainly our hope. If it doesn't go that way, our goal is that each departing team member be more competent, more capable, more polished, more seasoned, more articulate, and wiser than the day they walked in."

If you think about that for a minute, that's what love is all about, right? Love is about growing people. If your parents truly loved you, then they encouraged you to pursue your interests, and supported you materially (within reason!) and emotionally in those pursuits. Parents who truly love their child want to see that child learn, mature, develop, and grow. A boss who truly loves the people he or she works with wants the same thing.

Here's the dirty little secret: your people know whether you love them or not. It's really hard to fake. How do people know that you love them? You spend time with them, you coach them, you nurture them, you give them constructive feedback, you push them, you expect more of them than they expect of themselves, and you're willing to let them make mistakes so they can learn on their own. You're not overprotective. Just like parenting, sometimes you have to let people fail, because through failure we learn and grow.

If you spend no time with your people, take no interest in their success, don't know the names of their spouse or their children, and don't know where they went to college, that clearly communicates that

HOW DO PEOPLE KNOW THAT YOU LOVE THEM? YOU SPEND TIME WITH THEM, YOU COACH THEM, YOU NURTURE THEM, YOU GIVE THEM CONSTRUCTIVE FEEDBACK, YOU PUSH THEM, YOU EXPECT MORE OF THEM THAN THEY EXPECT OF THEMSELVES, AND YOU'RE WILLING TO LET THEM MAKE MISTAKES SO THEY CAN LEARN ON THEIR OWN.

you aren't very interested in them. What if you came home from school and your mom said, "Remind me what your name is again, and what grade you're in?"

A big job leaders have is to *de-hassle*. That means it's the leader's job to make it easier for their people to succeed. It doesn't mean doing the hard work for them. It means removing obstacles and barriers, the red tape and baloney politics that are typical in many companies, big and small. The leader's job is to reduce the amount of friction their people encounter so they can more easily do their jobs. If you remove barriers to their progress, coach and give them feedback, have empathy and communicate that empathy to them, and if you let them know you're there for support, it's amazing how far people can go and grow. There's a familiar saying, "People don't care how much you know until they know how much you care." It's true. If you don't love and care about your people, and you come in and try to teach them how to do something, they're going to dismiss it.

There's a question that's often asked in employee surveys: "How comfortable are you taking a problem to your manager?" The higher the response rate to that question, the more engaged that person is in the company. So, if that question were asked of your employees, and only 18 percent of the people in the company say, "I'm comfortable taking a problem to my manager," it means you don't have a very engaged workforce. Colin Powell famously said, "Leadership is solving problems. The day soldiers stop bringing you their problems is the day you have stopped leading them. They have either lost confidence that you can help or concluded you do not care. Either case is a failure of leadership."

Make no mistake: love is not expressed through perks, big salaries, or lots of fringe benefits, though that's what everybody thinks. For proof, look no further than wealthy parents who have given their children anything and everything they've ever wanted, and still have terrible relationships with their kids. It's not about giving your kid the new car that he wants when he turns sixteen, it's about going to your kid's basketball games from ages six to sixteen. Many people think they can buy their child's love. In business, it's so easy to think, "Oh, it's the money. If I paid him more, he'd be happy." That's a fallacy. You must be there for your team members, just as you must be there for your kids. When you create an environment in your company in which the leadership team cares about the people who work for them, word gets out. It creates a vibrant, supportive culture, one that will attract and retain the very best people.

WHEN YOU CREATE AN ENVIRONMENT IN YOUR COMPANY IN WHICH THE LEADERSHIP TEAM CARES ABOUT THE PEOPLE WHO WORK FOR THEM, WORD GETS OUT.

At Advantage, we're far from perfect on this. The dirty little secret is, you'll never be perfect. Even the best companies in the world are a work in progress. You must realize that creating an environment where your people say, "I'm looking forward to Monday," is a journey, not a destination. One of the greatest professional accolades we've received is being named one of the Best Places to Work in the state of South Carolina. To win this award, you have

YOU MUST REALIZE THAT CREATING AN ENVIRONMENT WHERE YOUR PEOPLE SAY, "I'M LOOKING FORWARD TO MONDAY," IS A JOURNEY, NOT A DESTINATION.

to apply, and then an independent group surveys your team members and essentially asks, "Off the record, is this a good company or a bad company?" Then, depending on the anonymous survey responses from each employee in each company, the companies are all ranked. Hundreds of companies apply every year, and no more than 50 make the list. We've made the list three separate times and into the top 20 twice! I take great pride in that, because it means we're doing a lot of things right. But we're not number one, and there have been years we haven't made the list. We're going to keep working until we make the list every year and we are number one, and when we become number one, we're going to have to keep working so we can stay number one.

The fun part is, it makes you a mini celebrity in your community. You're the CEO who has the company everybody wants to work for. People tell me, "Oh, I've heard so many great things about your business," or,

"I know somebody who works for you, and they gush about how much they love being there." If you've ever met a complete stranger who says, "Mike, I met your son, Jason, and let me tell you, what a polished, polite young professional he is—I was so impressed!"—you know much pride that brings. The same is true when you're a boss: "Hey, Mike, I just want to tell you, I ran into one of your colleagues, Amy, at a cocktail party last week. She wouldn't stop raving about what a great company Advantage is and how much she loves being there. Just thought you might want to know." If hearing something like that doesn't make your day, then you need to hang up your spurs and find a new profession!

You're in the people business. Every person has challenges and every person has baggage. A lot of people think, "Well, if the suitcase gets ugly, let's buy a new one." And indeed, if you get to a point with someone where the relationship is beyond repair, then you may need to replace the suitcase. However, by nature, people have problems—including you. Including me! It's life.

We have challenges like divorces, illnesses, and personal tragedies. When you hire team members, you're signing up for that journey with them. The truth is, if you're there for people when they need it, word gets out. If that person is truly an A-player, you're making an investment in them, and they won't forget you were there for them when they needed it. When you're there for them, not only do you engender their trust and goodwill, you're also raising your stock with everyone else in your company, because word will get around. Every team member knows that when one of their colleagues fell down, the company and the boss were there for them. The word gets out fast, and it makes a difference. Most people don't forget the person that brought them to the dance.

The CEO is the one who's responsible for promoting an attitude of love. If it doesn't come from the top, it's hard to accomplish. If every leader in the company loves their people, but the CEO despises them, then it just doesn't work. When you look at the greatest leaders in the world throughout history, whether they're business leaders, political leaders, or otherwise, there was ultimately a spirit of love that guided them. Abraham Lincoln, the man who united a divided nation, could've been unkind to the Confederate states, but instead, he forgave, reunified a country, and led with a spirit of love. Without Abraham Lincoln's spirit of love, we might well still be a house divided, and the United States of America would not be the beacon of hope and freedom for the world that it is today.

To be a world class leader, you must ultimately be a servant-leader. Being a servant-leader means putting the needs of others before your own, and it's impossible unless you truly love the people you're serving. There's an argument around the world as to whether leaders are born or made. There's no question

TO BE A WORLD CLASS LEADER, YOU MUST ULTIMATELY BE A SERVANT-LEADER. BEING A SERVANT-LEADER MEANS PUTTING THE NEEDS OF OTHERS BEFORE YOUR OWN, AND IT'S IMPOSSIBLE UNLESS YOU TRULY LOVE THE PEOPLE WHO YOU'RE SERVING.

there are certain innate traits we as people are born with; traits that predispose us to succeed in one thing or another. With that said, there is no doubt that leadership can be taught. These traits can be learned, they can be cultivated and they can be developed. I look at myself as a leader. Fifteen years ago, when I was an immature, inexperienced twenty-three-year-old kid who thought I could start a business, I would have rather watched paint dry than deal with the emotional needs of team members. I had the attitude of, "You're grown up. You're a big person. You can figure this out. I've paid you to come into my company, to be productive and work, not to come in and blab about your kids and be emotional. I pay you to get the job done." How immature I was!

I've developed. I've matured. I've grown. I've learned from others. I've learned from my own mistakes, and I've realized that if I embrace the attitude of love, success is much easier.

Ultimately, I had to get comfortable with myself, and embrace the fact that the real job of a leader is to build an organization with great people who are empowered to do great work. If you want to build a great company, you can't be the only one pulling the wagon. You must build a team of capable people to pull the wagon with you. That's what great leaders do. They inspire, they care for, and they enrich those who are pulling the wagon with them. As this book comes to a close, remember: Your job isn't to grow a company. Your job is to grow people who grow a company. When that happens, people really do look forward to Monday!

EPILOGUE

THE BUS
OF HAPP

NESS

NESS

"BUSINESS WAS ORIGINATED
TO PRODUCE HAPPINESS,
NOT TO PILE UP MILLIONS."

—B.C. FORBES

THE BUSINESS OF HAPPINESS

EARLIER IN THIS BOOK I TALKED

about how, in our company, our leadership team has three priorities. The first is team member happiness: we want to create an environment in which people can succeed, do great work, and be professionally fulfilled in the work they do. If we're successful at creating an atmosphere that makes our team members excited about coming to work on Mondays, we believe that will ultimately translate to profitable growth.

Yet the word "happiness" is a squishy word. In fact, it's so squishy if you walked up to ten people and asked them to define happiness, you'd almost certainly get ten different answers. And therein lies the challenge; if one of your goals is to create an environment where your people can be happy, yet nobody can define what happiness really is.

Over the last decade, we've hired quite a few people, and if I go back and look at the résumés we've received for all of those open positions, the total number exceeds ten thousand. At Advantage, that first stage of the hiring process is all done electronically, by filling out a questionnaire. One of the questions on our website is, "How do you define success?" Like happiness, I'll admit that "success" is another one of those squishy words; go back to those same ten people, ask them to define success, and I'm convinced you'll get ten different answers. Over the years I've spent a fair amount of time reviewing peoples' responses to that question, and you may not be surprised to learn that of the ten thousand responses, the number one answer to that question is: "to be happy." That word again! But what do they really mean—and how could I address that desire as a leader?

That led me to a deep dive into what drives happiness for most people, and I've boiled it down to six key elements. If you're a CEO or an entrepreneur that wants to create a world-class organization, knowing what these are gives you a tremendous leg up. If you understand these six drivers of happiness and can create an environment that brings those things to the people in your organization, you have a powerful formula that allows you to foster happiness within your organization. Let's break down those six drivers of happiness, and explore their applications in the working environment.

IF YOU UNDERSTAND THESE SIX DRIVERS OF HAPPINESS AND CAN CREATE AN ENVIRONMENT THAT BRINGS THOSE THINGS TO THE PEOPLE IN YOUR ORGANIZATION, YOU HAVE A POWERFUL FORMULA THAT ALLOWS YOU TO FOSTER HAPPINESS WITHIN YOUR ORGANIZATION.

. . . .

THE SIX DRIVERS OF HAPPINESS

The first is **learning and growing**. In my observation, when people are actively engaged in learning and growing, they're typically happy. And if you think about that for a minute, it makes perfect sense, because if we're not growing, we're dying; there's no in between. When we're acquiring new skills, learning about new subjects, and absorbing knowledge and information that make us more competent and capable, that tends to put a smile on our face, because we know that increased skills and competency make us more valuable. It doesn't matter whether that value is in gaining the skills needed to get the promotion we've worked hard for—or in improving our parenting skills, or learning to be a better listener with our spouse—when we're learning and growing as an individual, it's deeply satisfying.

Recognizing that, as a CEO I'm constantly asking myself what we as a company can do to help our team members learn and grow. If, over the course of a year, the people in our company can look back over their accomplishments and see real professional growth, it helps to drive their happiness.

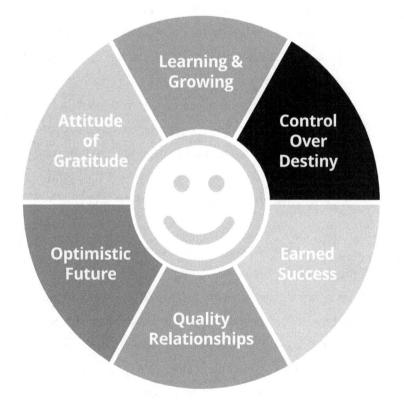

The 6 Drivers of Happiness

The second driver of happiness I've identified is **having control over your destiny**. We all want to captain our own ship. There's no doubt that when people feel they are in control of their destiny and can directly influence their outcomes, they're going to be happier. In a historical context, you might say that's one of the reasons that capitalism has triumphed over socialism. In socialism, the cake is essentially baked. No matter how hard you work, no matter how hard you try, everybody has the same outcome, whereas in capitalism (and despite its imperfections), there's the implicit promise that if you work hard, if you apply yourself, if you make smart choices and smart decisions, you can control your destiny and create your own success. Whatever success looks like to you, it's within your grasp if you work for it. But when you feel you have no control—that no matter what you do, it won't matter—you're in a hopeless and depleted state, and that saps whatever ambition or creativity you might have.

That's why it's essential to create a work environment in which people have control over their destiny. At Advantage that translates to helping our team members set goals professionally and provide them with the resources to achieve those goals. This enables them to create their own career path, chart their progress along the way, and take pride in the results.

HELPING OUR TEAM MEMBERS SET GOALS PROFESSIONALLY AND GIVING THEM THE RESOURCES TO ACHIEVE THOSE GOALS ENABLES THEM TO CREATE THEIR OWN CAREER PATH, CHART THEIR PROGRESS ALONG THE WAY, AND TAKE PRIDE IN THE RESULTS."

. . . .

That leads us to the third driver of happiness, which is in a way an outcome of the previous—what we call **earned success**. Earned success is simply setting a goal or an objective and achieving it. This leads to tremendous satisfaction, whether it's personal or professional. Think of the times you've resolved to improve your health, whether that meant running a marathon, losing weight, or getting to the gym on a regular schedule. Setting your goal and hitting it brings fulfillment and a sense of personal accomplishment.

And it's the same in a professional context. Maybe you've been asked to give an important presentation, or lead a project team. When that presentation has been successfully delivered, or your project effectively completed, and the CEO of the company personally seeks you out to tell you how impressed he or she was with the work you did, that's a hugely gratifying feeling. That's why helping your people set their goals, giving them resources to succeed in hitting those goals, and recognizing their successes is something that a company can do to positively impact workplace happiness.

The fourth driver is **quality relationships**. People that are the happiest, I have found, are those that enjoy productive relationships—both personal and professional—with their family, colleagues, and friends. When people have high quality relationships, they're happy, because happy relationships are largely drama-free. There's no gossip. There's no backstabbing. There isn't the trepidation of, "Oh, no, I've got to go to Thanksgiving this year and my awful mother-in-law is going to be there."

When you have productive relationships personally and professionally, it leads to happiness. As CEOs and business leaders, we can't do much about the quality of the relationship those in our company have with their mothers-in-law, but we certainly can teach skills that can help them to improve *all* of their relationships. Communication skills, listening skills, and empathy skills all have an impact on the quality of relationships you have with others in any sphere. And we can build in opportunities for the people on our team to interact in positive ways and communicate better with each other.

The fifth driver of happiness is **having an optimistic future**. When you feel that your best days are still ahead of you, it creates a sense of excitement and positive anticipation. Alternately, when you've got nothing to look forward to, when you're convinced that your best days are behind you, and life is nothing but a downhill ride going forward—that's a bleak outlook. That's why I think it's so important for a company to help craft career path plans with their people; so they can see a fruitful future for themselves. Show them what's possible—where their efforts and energy can take them—and give them a concrete reason to be optimistic and happy.

The sixth and final driver of happiness is **gratitude**. At first that might surprise you or seem out of place but hear me out. Many years ago, I was listening to a speaker at a conference I was attending. The speaker said "if you spend the rest of your life comparing up, you will always be disappointed. If you spend the rest of your life comparing down, you will always be grateful." I thought about if further. She was right. There will always be someone with more money, a bigger business, a bigger house, a nicer car, a more attractive spouse. When you compare up, it is easy to feel disappointed and inadequate. I've found that I'm most happy when I have a "attitude of gratitude." Yep, I spend three minutes each day, right before I go to bed, reminding myself how lucky I am and how grateful

I am for all that I have. Those that are most grateful are also the most happy. As a CEO or leader, you can do things in your business to foster gratitude. To start, begin regularly expressing to your team members the gratitude you feel their contributions. You might just find a tipping point in your business.

At the end of the day, if you have a team of happy people, you're going to see the results in the top line, in the bottom line, and in your company's ability to achieve its goals. To me, the imperative of the CEO is to create a team of people that are happy, engaged, and fulfilled; to give them a strategic plan, to help them understand how the work they do moves that plan forward—and then set them free.

Try it. You'll be amazed at how far they—and you—can go.

IF YOU HAVE A TEAM
OF HAPPY PEOPLE,
YOU'RE GOING TO
SEE THE RESULTS IN
THE TOP LINE, IN THE
BOTTOM LINE, AND
IN YOUR COMPANY'S
ABILITY TO ACHIEVE
ITS GOALS.

THE JOURNEY BEGINS....

CONGRATULATIONS!

You've finished this book. Give yourself a pat on the back. Now, realize the fact that you've read this book doesn't mean squat if you don't act on the things you've learned. This book is meant to be a teaching tool. This book is meant to provide a few ideas and a partial roadmap you can follow. However, the hard work has only begun.

It's a long and arduous journey to create an environment that makes your team say, "I'm looking forward to Monday," but I assure you, it's worth the effort. Just like self-improvement, the journey you're about to embark on is one that has no endpoint. The true joy of taking the *Looking Forward to Monday* journey is the journey itself, not the destination. You'll never quite get there, but the person you'll become and the company you'll create will be far better than it would have been had you opted to pull over and park on the side of the road.

The rewards are many: stronger business performance, quicker growth, bigger top-line revenues, and fatter bottom-line profits. But more gratifying than any of these will be the personal fulfillment and joy that you, the leader, will receive by taking your company down this road and through this process—and that fulfillment and joy you experience will spill over to your entire team and throughout your whole life.

I've always believed the role of servant-leader is the most noble of all, because you can make a difference in people's lives in a big way. If you have twenty-five team members in your company, and those twenty-five people have spouses and children, then you'll have a significant impact on the lives of, say, one hundred individuals. If you have a company of 250 people, you may have a significant impact on the lives of 1,000 people or more, and that doesn't include other entrepreneurs who will see what you're doing and be inspired and motivated by it. That doesn't include the city and community where your business is based that will be in awe of what you've achieved. It creates a ripple effect that just keeps going.

At the end of your career, will you look back and say, "I made a difference"? Will others look at you and say, "Well done, good and faithful servant"? I believe every person on this earth has a purpose, and the purpose of servant-leaders is to make a difference in the lives of their team members by empowering, equipping, and educating them to serve the world with their unique purpose.

Let's get started!

RESOURCES

Adams, Susan. "Most Americans Are Unhappy At Work." *Forbes.* last modified June 20, 2014. https://www.forbes.com/sites/susanadams/2014/06/20/most-americans-are-unhappy-at-work/#34587b50341a.

"BHAG—Big, Hairy, Audacious Goal."Jim Collins. http://www.jimcollins.com/article_topics/articles/BHAG.html.

Merhar, Christina. "Employee Retention-The Real Cost of Losing an Employee." *ZaneBenefits.* last modified February 4, 2016 https://www.zanebenefits.com/blog/bid/312123/employee-retention-the-real-cost-of-losing-an-employee.

SUGGESTED READING

Hyper Sales Growth: Street-Proven Systems & Processes. How to Grow Quickly & Profitably by Jack Daly

Scaling Up: How a Few Companies Make It...and Why the Rest Don't (Rockefeller Habits 2.0) by Verne Harnish

Who: The Method for Hiring by Geoff Smart

American Icon: Alan Mulally and the Fight to Save Ford Motor Company by Bryce Hoffman

Good to Great: Why Some Companies Make the Leap and Others Don't by Jim Collins

Nuts!: Southwest Airlines' Crazy Recipe for Business and Personal Success by Kevin Freiberg and Jackie Freiberg

Relentless Implementation: Creating Clarity, Alignment, and a Working Together Operating System to Maximize Your Business Performance by Alan Mulally and Adam Witty

ABOUT THE AUTHOR

ADAM WITTY IS THE FOUNDER AND CEO of Advantage, the Business Growth Company. What began in the spare bedroom of his home is now a family of publishing, media, and software businesses that collectively serve thousands of customers in fifty US states and sixty-seven countries.

The Advantage Family includes Advantage|ForbesBooks, one of the largest independent business book publishers in the world; BusinessAdvantage TV, a video-on-demand learning platform for entrepreneurs; Magnetic Marketing, a marketing education company for entrepreneurs; BPR 360, business operating software for entrepreneurs; and mLive, multi-step marketing automation software for dentists.

Adam was named to the prestigious Inc. 30 Under 30 list of America's Coolest Entrepreneurs in 2011. Advantage has been named to the Inc. 500/5000 list for six of the past eight years. Adam is the author of nine books and has appeared in *USA Today*, *Investor's Business Daily*, and *The Wall Street Journal*, and on ABC and FOX. Adam is a leading expert globally on

"Authority Marketing" and he coauthored the best-selling book *Authority Marketing* with Rusty Shelton. Adam's book, *Book the Business: How to Make Big Money With Your Book Without Even Selling a Single Copy,* was coauthored with marketing legend Dan Kennedy. Adam's most recent book, *Relentless Implementation,* was coauthored with Alan Mulally, retired CEO of Boeing Commercial Airplanes and Ford Motor Company.

Adam is the publisher of *Authority Magazine* and *ForbesBooks Review Magazine.* Adam is an Eagle Scout, pilot, member of EO and YPO, and past board chair of Clemson University's Spiro Entrepreneurship Institute and nonprofit Youth Entrepreneurship South Carolina. Adam was named Charleston's 2019 Entrepreneur of the Year by the Harbor Entrepreneur Center.